THE COMPLETE MULTIENGINE PILOT

by

Robert E. Gardner

Original Artwork

by Richard Bringloe

asa Aviation Supplies & Academics, Inc. / Renton, Washington

The Complete Multiengine Pilot

© 1989, 1990 by ASA

All rights reserved, including the right to reproduce this book or any portions thereof in any form.

PRINTED IN THE UNITED STATES OF AMERICA

ISBN 0-940732-92-0

asa

Aviation Supplies & Academics, Inc.
7005 132nd Place SE
Renton, Washington 98059-9236

TABLE OF CONTENTS

ACKNOWLEGEMENT v

CHAPTER ONE
    Introduction to Twins .... 1-1 thru 1-2

CHAPTER TWO
    The Concept of Multiengine Flying .... 2-1 thru 2-6

CHAPTER THREE
    Multiengine Airplane Systems .... 3-1 thru 3-19

CHAPTER FOUR
    Planning and Performance .... 4-1 thru 4-18

CHAPTER FIVE
    Takeoff and Departure .... 5-1 thru 5-8

CHAPTER SIX
    Cruising Flight .... 6-1 thru 6-5

CHAPTER SEVEN
    Descent, Approach and Landing .... 7-1 thru 7-6

CHAPTER EIGHT
    Preparing for a Multiengine Checkride .... 8-1 thru 8-8

APPENDICES

    A — Glossary .... A-1 thru A-2

    B — Practical Test Standards .... B-1 thru B-50
        (Airplane Multiengine Land)

        Practical Test Checklist (AMEL) .... B-51 thru B-53

    C — Index .... C-1 thru C-2

Acknowledgement

As an aviation educator, I have amassed quite a collection of books, magazines, audio tapes and videotapes. I have subscribed to just about every aviation publication available during the past 20 years, and I can't visit a pilot supply store without buying at least one book. My library includes a wide variety of Federal publications available to the public and some that I have scrounged from friends in the FAA.

I must admit, then, that the methods and procedures discussed in this book are not new, unique or original; with the exception of the zero-sideslip theory, there is nothing new in the aerodynamics of multiengine flight and the handling of emergencies. This text is a synthesis of the ideas of many authors as I have absorbed them over the years, molded and shaped by my own experience as a pilot and instructor. My thanks to all of the pilot-authors whose words and thoughts have contributed to this book.

I am fortunate that Les Berven, the FAA engineer whose research on zero sideslip forced changes in multiengine training, is based right here in Seattle. Mr. Berven has checked the text to be sure that it accurately reflects his findings and has contributed invaluable information based on his experience as a test pilot and engineer.

CHAPTER ONE

INTRODUCTION TO TWINS

ART BLANSTER'S SIX-PASSENGER SINGLE-engine airplane is sleek, fast, and equipped with the latest in navigation equipment, but it is uncomfortably close to its maximum gross takeoff weight when he loads it with his business associates and the equipment they need to make a sales demonstration in a distant city. A multiengine airplane will give Art the load-carrying capability that he needs. Adding "Multiengine Land" to his certificate is a business necessity.

Paula Forsham's flying club has six singles and a twin, and she is checked out in every one of the single-engine airplanes. Six months ago, a vacuum pump failure in one of them resulted in a descent through clouds using needle, ball and airspeed, and just last week a broken alternator belt caused a total electrical failure. Paula is aware that a twin's redundant vacuum and electrical systems will tip the odds in her favor.

Pat Manley is 21 and has already logged 1,400 hours in single engine airplanes as an instructor and charter pilot. He wants to put a multiengine Airline Transport Pilot certificate in his wallet when he turns 23, and he knows that the more twin time he has in his log, the better his chances with a commuter or major airline will be. For Pat, getting a twin rating is a smart career move.

Each of these pilots accepts the fact that getting a Multiengine rating will involve added costs, but they all feel that the advantages outweigh the disadvantages. Each pilot will rationalize the decision to upgrade in his or her own way, but there is no denying that having Multiengine Land added to a pilot's certificate gives that pilot the extra pride of accomplishment that goes with stepping up to a higher skill level. Paula, Pat, and Art are ready to take on a new challenge — are you?

Multiengine Training

The FAA does not require that you log a minimum number of hours of instruction before the multiengine checkride. The flight check is a demonstration of proficiency, and your instructor will recommend you for the checkride when he or she feels that you are ready. During training, you will probably spend an hour or two doing airwork, such as slow flight, approaches to stalls, and steep turns, to develop a sense of how an airplane with more of its mass off-center behaves. Pattern work will consist of normal takeoffs and landings as well as short and soft field takeoffs and landings. Then the focus of attention will shift to emergencies, both at altitude and close to the surface. You can hone some of the required skills in a good multiengine simulator at a considerable reduction in cost and total time to checkride proficiency. Although skill levels of pilots and instructors vary, figure that five hours is a questionably short course and that twenty hours of airplane time is overkill.

No written examination is required for the multiengine rating, but you can expect to be grilled on your trainer's performance numbers and operational systems by your instructor, by the examiner who gives you the checkride and by anyone from whom you rent a similar twin. Thorough knowledge of any multiengine airplane's operating systems is required.

That is an outline of what you are getting into, as far as flying goes. Now let's talk about this book.

Isn't it true that almost all of your one-on-one education as a pilot took place before you received your Private Pilot certificate, when new information and experiences were a part of every flight lesson? Except for being checked out in different singles, have you had many opportunities to sit down with an instructor and go over how the aeronautical facts of life you learned as a student pilot apply to larger, more powerful aircraft? As a multiengine pilot, your safety and that of your passengers will depend on your full understanding of the aerodynamic laws that govern flight in a twin when one engine is not delivering power. This book is intended to serve as that one-on-one talk.

Dual systems? Sure, but they offer more variables than you have been exposed to in single-

engine airplanes. You need a thorough grasp of how these systems work, what they can do for you, and how they are affected by an engine failure. This book will dig more deeply into systems than did your basic texts.

What will the examiner look for on your checkride? To what new experiences will your multiengine instructor expose you? What new elements of flight planning will a multiengine airplane require? We'll go through each of these subjects together, with the goal of making you a knowledgeable multiengine pilot.

Other than having an extra engine, how does a twin differ from the airplanes you have been flying? We'll discuss that first, with special attention to operating systems, then we will look into the planning considerations. From there, we will go into a normal takeoff and climb, cruise considerations, approach planning, and the landing. All-engine and engine-out procedures are discussed in each section. We'll take a look at the FAA Practical Test Standards for the multiengine rating and talk about how to prepare for each area of operation and task.

From the earliest hours of your private pilot training you were asked, "Where would you put it if the engine failed?" Your job was to find a suitable landing site within gliding distance, and you didn't have to fight to control the airplane on the way. When one engine quits on a twin, however, control is your paramount concern. That is why your training — and this book — will concentrate heavily on what to do if an engine fails, why the failure causes control problems, and how following the correct procedures will make the airplane easier to control.

CHAPTER TWO

THE CONCEPT OF MULTIENGINE FLYING

WHY DOES A MULTIENGINE AIRPLANE NEED two engines? Because it won't fly on one, that's why. To understand that statement, the significant factor is "pounds per horsepower," which relates to the amount of weight that a given engine can haul into the air at sea level on a standard day. If you want to lift more pounds, you must either install a larger engine or add an engine, and there are practical limits as to just how big a single engine can be for a given airframe. Big engines require lots of room and a plentiful source of cooling air, which translates into a large cowling with equally large frontal area. That, in turn, adds drag, and pretty soon you defeat the original purpose. Often, the best solution is a second engine.

The Piper Seneca (figure 2-1 on next page) is an excellent example of a manufacturer adding a second engine to an existing airframe. Its ancestor, the Cherokee Six, with a single 300-horsepower engine, is able to carry seven people and has capacious baggage compartments. The Seneca I (the original, non-turbocharged model) was a Cherokee Six airframe with two engines. It didn't offer much in the way of additional useful load, but it did provide two-engine safety. Other examples of singles that became twins when they grew up are the Twin Comanche and the Twin Bonanza.

The gain that is achieved by adding an engine is in excess horsepower. Every airplane derives its ability to climb from excess horsepower; excess, that is, to the amount of power required to sustain level flight. You typically choose a cruise power setting which keeps power in reserve, ready for use when called upon, instead of pushing all of the levers full forward. Those extra horses would, if summoned to action,

Figure 2-1. Piper Seneca II

provide either greater level flight speed or climb capability. As you climb to higher altitudes, and the power output of the engines decreases, the ability to climb also decreases.

Figure 2-2 illustrates how total drag varies with airspeed. Its components are induced drag, which is greatest at low speed and diminishes as speed increases, and parasitic drag, which is negligible at low speed but increases with the square of airspeed. The minimum total drag point (the bottom of the curve) is very close to the single-engine best rate-of-climb speed, which is achieved, in this illustration, at 40 percent power.

As you can see, there is plenty of excess power to the right of the minimum drag point as long as both engines are running. When the power of one engine is not available, however, only the power in the shaded portion of the graph is available. High density altitude or a "good" engine which, for one reason or another, is not putting out full rated power, will cause the shaded area to shrink.

During the first hour or so of multiengine training, you and your instructor can perform an experiment that will prove how the excess horsepower pays off. Trim your aircraft to maintain level flight at its best rate-of-climb speed and record the power setting; then, without touching the throttle or trim wheel, pull back on the control yoke and wait. For a few moments, the kinetic energy of the airplane's forward motion will allow it to climb — but it won't last. Because the increased angle of attack adds to induced drag, the airspeed will slowly decrease and the airplane will begin to descend. After a few oscillations, it will stabilize at the original altitude. You have established the minimum power required to maintain altitude. Now go back to the original situation (trimmed for level flight at Vy) and add power; the aircraft will climb as a result of power in excess of that required to sustain level flight. It should be apparent that if an engine fails, erasing one-half of the total power, there will be little excess power available for climbing.

To prove how the loss of excess power hurts performance, repeat your earlier experiment but this time trim to maintain the single-engine best rate-of-climb speed (Vyse, or the blue line on the airspeed indicator) in level flight. Pull one throttle back to zero thrust (about 12 inches of manifold pressure is a good approximation) and do whatever is necessary to the remaining engine to avoid losing altitude. You will find that the "good" engine is producing 75 percent power or more, and that pushing it up to maximum power may result in a very modest rate of climb. The effect of the loss of power in excess of that necessary for level flight will be obvious.

That, then, is the concept of multiengine flight — add a second engine, and as long as both are humming the same tune, you will have copious amounts of excess horsepower to convert into cruising speed or climb capability if temperature, pressure altitude, and weight are within reasonable limits. That's the good news.

The bad news is that your multiengine flight training will place disproportionate emphasis on engine failures — disproportionate, that is, to the chances of your ever experiencing a total power loss on one engine. All instructors know that placing emphasis on the negative aspects of a subject is a poor teaching technique, and it is with reluctance that they devote more time to the hazards of multiengine flight than to its successes. What they know, and what you should read into their instruction and into this text, is that multiengine airplanes can be controlled when only one engine is running *if* the pilot knows what to do, how to do it, and why it is being done — and has the presence of mind to do the right thing when the situation demands it. When your friends show you statistics on multiengine accidents, point out that there are no statistics on how many twins experienced problems but landed without incident.

When both engines are purring in sweet harmony, a twin doesn't fly any differently than any sleek single-engine retractable. If the single engine of that retractable quits, however, the failure does not create control problems. You have little choice but to find the safest, least expensive spot to put it down. A second engine provides you with options, depending on where you are when the failure occurs. Some wags have said that it takes you to the scene of the accident. Realistically, once you have gained control of the airplane after an engine failure, the odds are very much in your favor.

The FAA doesn't require that a multiengine airplane weighing less than 6,000 pounds be able to climb or even maintain altitude on one engine; its only requirement is that the plane be controllable as it gradually sinks earthward. When you hear the phrase "light twin," remember that 6,000-pound limit. However, almost all light twins are able to climb at least minimally on one engine. The Champion Lancer, a fabric-covered, fixed-gear twin, is known for its inability to maintain altitude when one of its little engines quits. Airplanes heavier than 6,000 pounds (or which stall at a speed higher than 61 knots) must demonstrate the ability to climb on one engine at 5,000 feet above sea level, and that means either more horsepower or turbocharging.

Beginning Your Multiengine Training

When you first learned to fly, your relationship with your instructor was clear-cut; the instructor took over control of the airplane whenever a situation began to deteriorate. You were a novice, your instructor was a professional, and "I've

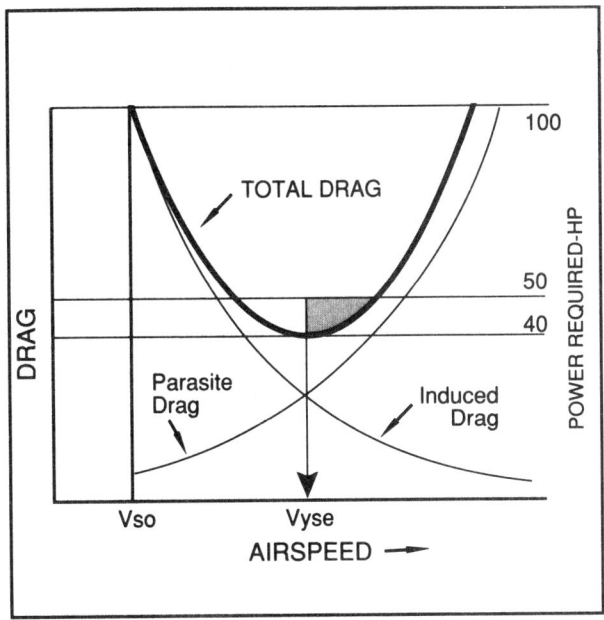

Figure 2-2. Drag vs airpeed

got it!" was your signal to let go of everything. When you begin your multiengine instruction, the situation will change. You are now an experienced pilot, and until your instructor decides that it is time to begin failing engines, he or she will place responsibility for normal operations in your hands. Unfortunately, the airplane doesn't know that this comfortable situation exists, and it may decide to test the reactions of the entire front-seat crew. From the first takeoff, then, there should be complete understanding of who is in charge of the airplane if something out of the ordinary occurs. There have been many incidents in which each pilot thought the other was in control, and just as many in which both pilots were trying to fly the airplane at the same time.

Instructional flight has the highest rate of accidents after engine failure, and for good reason. One proficient pilot can handle an engine-out emergency alone, and a crew of two with specific emergency duties assigned can handle a failed engine without it turning into an accident. With an instructor and multiengine student occupying the front seats, however, confusion can result. The instructor wants to see how far into a situation the student can go without losing control, and the student feels that the in-

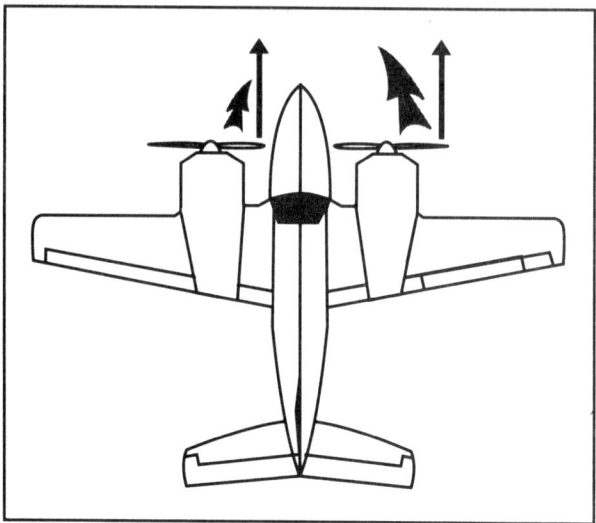

Figure 2-3. Yaw force due to P-factor

structor will bail him or her out before things get dicey.

Each occupant of a pilot seat should have a clear understanding of his or her responsibilities as the throttles are pushed forward. By now I hope that you are asking, "What is so different about having one of the engines fail on a multiengine airplane?" The answer lies in some aerodynamic laws that you are already aware of.

What Happens When an Engine Fails

When you practiced steep turns as a student pilot, you learned that if one wing is moving faster than the other, the lift imbalance will cause the airplane to roll toward the slower wing; you called it "overbanking tendency" then. You also learned about P-factor, the force created by the descending propeller blade that causes left-turning tendency in single-engine airplanes. And your instructor admonished you to use rudder when rolling into a turn to offset the drag created by a downward-deflected aileron. All of these elements will be present as we consider the effect of engine failure.

Basically, when an engine fails on a twin, its wing is no longer being pulled forward and the opposite wing begins to move faster; the resulting yaw develops a rolling moment toward the dead engine. P-factor comes into play as the pilot increases the pitch attitude to avoid losing altitude. Finally, the windmilling propeller on the ailing engine creates drag of much greater magnitude than a deflected aileron. Put all of these reactions together, and you can visualize why the airplane rolls and turns toward the failed engine, and why, if the pilot does not act quickly and correctly, the airplane might hit the ground in a steep bank or inverted. It doesn't have to happen, and your training will give you confidence in your ability to handle such an emergency if your skills are kept sharp. In later chapters, we will go into detail about what to do and why you do it.

Multiengine Aerodynamics

Figure 2-3 shows the forces at work when both engines are operating. There is no imbalance in either thrust or lift. The propellers on both engines rotate clockwise as seen from the cockpit, so the descending blades on the right side of the propeller discs are doing most of the work. However, note that the left engine's descending blade is much closer to the centerline of the fuselage than is the descending blade on the right engine. If the right engine fails, the yawing force exerted by the left engine's P-factor will be rela-

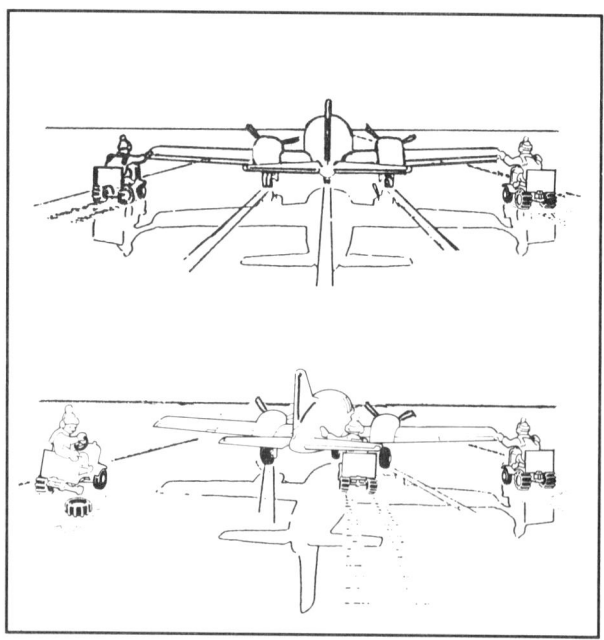

Figure 2-4. Forces acting on the airplane

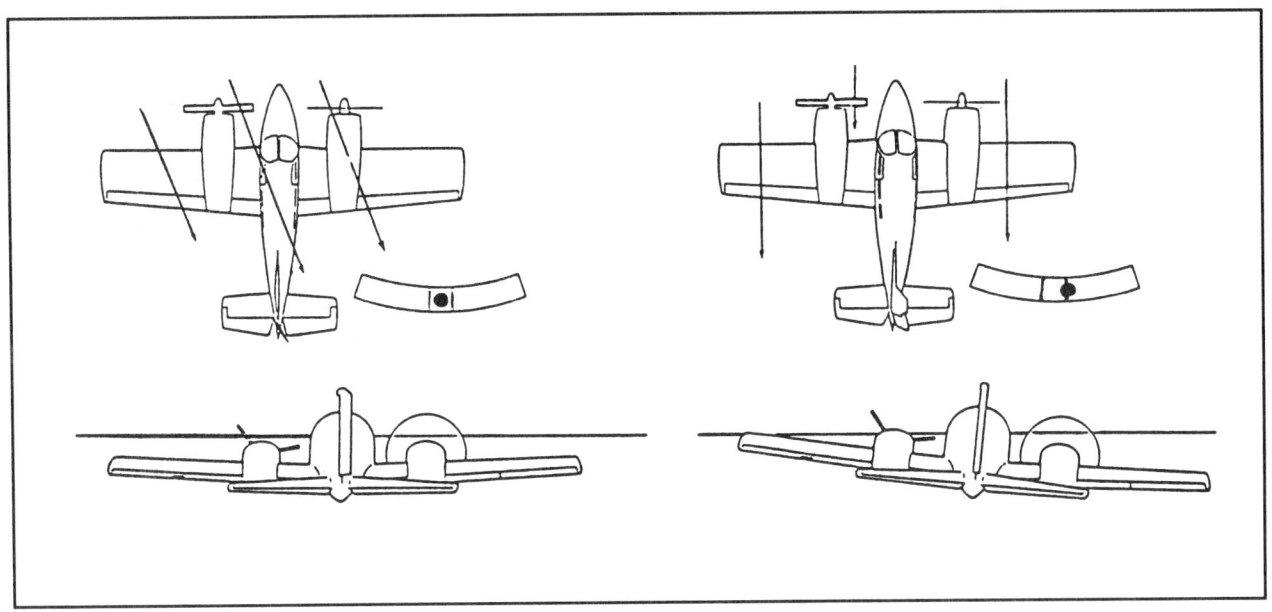

Figure 2-5. Horizontal component of lift provides force to correct sideslip

tively small, as indicated by the little arrow. If the left engine fails, however, the force exerted by the right engine's descending blade will be farther from the centerline and the yawing force will be much greater; the large arrow emphasizes the difference. The left engine is called the critical engine; its failure would create the most control problems for the pilot.

Many modern multiengine airplanes have counter-rotating propellers — the right engine's propeller rotates counterclockwise, so that the descending blades of both engines are equidistant from the centerline and P-factor cancels out. There is no critical engine. This reduces, but does not eliminate, the problems associated with controlling the airplane on one engine.

To illustrate how an engine failure causes a yaw and roll toward the dead engine, first look at figure 2-4 in which the thrust developed by the engines is represented by airplane tugs. (Since airplane tugs can't get much traction when airborne, the airplane in the illustration is on the ramp and cannot be banked.) The forces on the wings are balanced, and the airplane moves forward in a straight line. However, if one tug loses a wheel and stops pulling, the force of the other tug pulling its wing forward will cause the airplane to turn toward the dead tug. If a third tug rushes to the rescue and pushes on the good tug side of the fuselage, the turning motion can be arrested. Imagine all of this activity taking place in the dead of winter with the ramp covered with ice; the airplane will move in a direction determined partly by the tug on the right wing and partly by the tug pushing on the fuselage, as you can see in the picture.

Replace the two wingtip tugs with engine thrust and the fuselage tug with a fully deflected rudder, and you can see why an airplane with one engine inoperative and its wings level is slipping toward the dead engine. The relative wind blows against the side of the fuselage and the resultant drag increase is significant. There is no way to bring the relative wind into alignment with the centerline of the fuselage as long as the wings are level.

Get the airplane airborne, however, and a new stabilizing force becomes available: the horizontal component of lift that is developed when the wings are banked. On the left side of figure 2-5, control surface deflection replaces the forces exerted by the tugs in figure 2-4, and the resultant motion is indicated by the arrows. When the wings are level, a vertical lift vector is developed, and the magnitude of that vector is equal to the weight of the airplane. As you begin to

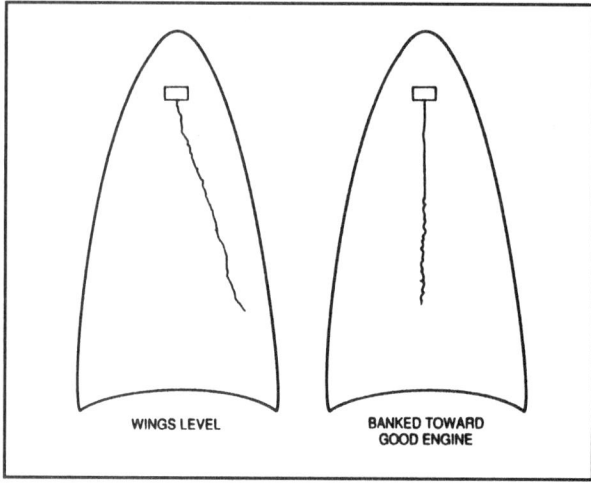

Figure 2-6.

roll the airplane, the vertical lift vector shrinks (and you must increase the angle of attack to maintain altitude), and a horizontal lift component is developed which increases in proportion to the angle of bank. At a 90-degree bank angle, there would be no vertical lift vector and the airplane would fall out of the sky.

So much for reviewing turn dynamics. By banking toward the good engine (figure 2-5, right) you can develop a horizontal lift vector that will, in effect, provide a correcting force so that the airplane will fly forward without any appreciable degree of sideslip. You could, theoretically, bank steeply enough that the horizontal component of force would make rudder deflection unnecessary. Of course, at liftoff and initial climb speeds, it is not possible to maintain altitude if you bank that steeply. Note the position of the ball on each side of figure 2-5. With the wings level and the airplane slipping toward the dead engine, trimming the ball into the center is the wrong answer. FAA experiments have shown that a pilot can lose control of the airplane at airspeeds as much as 15 knots higher than the minimum control speed marked on the airspeed indicator if the wings are level with the ball centered. Minimum control speed (Vmc) will be discussed in detail in Chapter Four.

Figure 2-6 illustrates the use of a yaw string, taped to the nose of the airplane and free to stream with the relative wind. The string streams toward the good engine side with the wings level, and becomes aligned with the longitudinal axis when the airplane is banked into the good engine, graphically illustrating zero sideslip.

To achieve the book Vmc figure at the moment of failure, you must establish a bank angle of at least (not at most) 5 degrees toward the good engine and let the ball move about one diameter toward the good engine. In this situation the attitude indicator is not a reliable bank indicator and you must use the ball as a bank indicator rather than as a slip/skid indicator. A precise 5 degree bank duplicates the conditions under which the manufacturer determined minimum controllable airspeed to meet FAA certification requirements (with sophisticated instrumentation that is not found in production airplanes), but it means nothing to a pilot struggling to maintain control of a crippled airplane.

Banking 5 or more degrees toward the good engine cuts into climb capability, so when you have the airplane under control, you should reduce the bank angle until the ball is deflected halfway out of the center for best performance. Note on page B-47, that the Practical Test Standards do not specify a bank angle but ask you to establish a bank that will result in maximum climb performance. Although you should not be doing math problems in your head during an emergency, you can make a fair approximation of the optimum engine-out bank angle with this formula, which uses numbers readily available in your Pilot's Operating Handbook and can be calculated in advance for each twin you fly: The sine of the optimum bank angle is 1/3 of the horsepower to weight ratio. For example, the maximum gross takeoff weight of an Aztec F is 5200 pounds, and each engine is rated at 250 horsepower. The ratio of engine-out horsepower to weight is 5200 v 250 = .048, and one-third of that figure is .016. From a book of trigonometric functions, .0175 is the sine of 1 degree, so the optimum bank angle for that model is hardly measurable. On a typical training flight, the airplane will be considerably lighter than max gross and the optimum bank angle will increase slightly. Your best bet during training is to have your instructor secure the critical engine (if the airplane has one) with the propeller feathered, experiment with bank angles into the good engine until you get the best reading on the vertical speed indicator, and then note the ball position.

You could take advantage of this situation to determine zero thrust by adjusting the good engine controls to establish level flight at V_{yse} and then bringing the failed engine back on line. When its throttle and propeller controls are adjusted to re-establish level flight, you will have duplicated the feathered-prop conditions as closely as possible and can use these zero-thrust settings for the rest of your training.

That lays the theoretical foundation for the actions you will take in an engine-out emergency. In later chapters, we will discuss just what you should do if an engine fails during takeoff and initial climb, during cruise, or during the descent and approach to land.

CHAPTER THREE

MULTIENGINE AIRPLANE SYSTEMS

AS THE PILOT OF A MULTIENGINE AIRPLANE, YOU will have more systems to learn and understand than you ever had to contend with in a single-engine airplane, because of duplication. It's great to have two alternators sharing the electrical load, but not quite so great when one alternator is out of action because its engine has failed and you have to throw the correct switches and pull the proper breakers to keep from overloading the sole survivor. And it's great to have lots of fuel to feed the engines — but not quite so great when a pump fails and you must know how to get fuel to the engines without that pump. But don't despair; all that is necessary is a little study and some judicious questioning of a friendly mechanic. Let's start by discussing systems that are unique to twins.

Propeller Feathering

If you have flown an airplane with a constant-speed propeller, you know that the propeller hub contains a governor that keeps the propeller's rotational speed constant by varying the pitch of the blades. The terms "pitch" and "blade angle" are used interchangeably, although they describe different things. The pitch of a propeller blade, expressed in inches, is the theoretical distance that the propeller moves forward through the air during one revolution (without slippage). Blade angle is the angle between the chord of the propeller blade and the plane of rotation. Because changes in blade angle cause changes in pitch, little confusion results from interchanging the two terms.

The most efficient angle of attack for a propeller is 2 to 4 degrees, and the actual blade angle necessary to maintain this small angle of attack varies with the forward speed of the airplane. Figure 3-1 on the following page illustrates the forces involved. The forward velocity vector is shortened and lengthened as the airplane gains or loses airspeed; the governor wants to keep

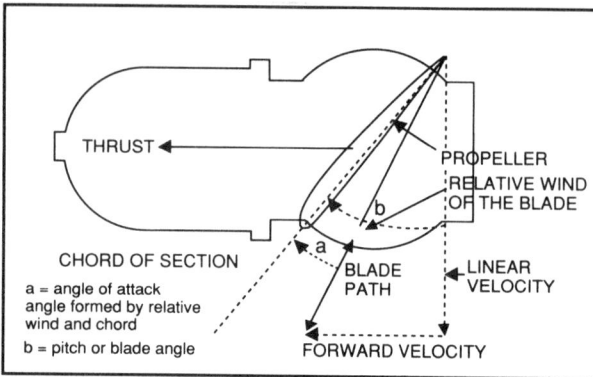

Figure 3-1. Propeller forces

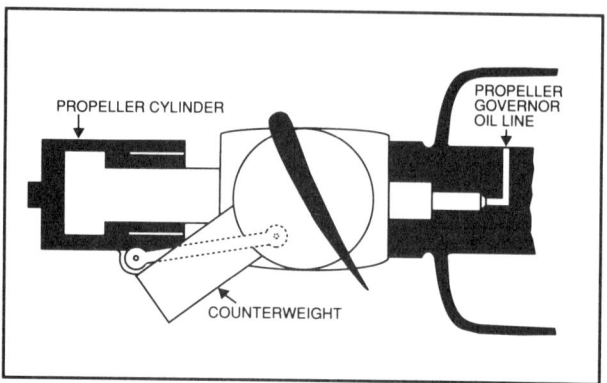

Figure 3-2. Pitch mechanism

the blade angle constant. If the angle of attack "a" is to stay within the efficient range, the blade angle "b" must be reduced (higher RPM) when forward velocity slows, and increased (lower RPM) when forward velocity accelerates. That is the function of the governor.

In the prop hub of some single-engine airplanes, the governor uses oil from the engine's lubricating system to force the propeller blades toward the low pitch (high RPM) position, and if oil pressure is lost due to engine stoppage, the blades are automatically moved to a high pitch or low RPM setting by counterweights (see figure 3-2). Other governing systems use oil pressure to move the blades to the high pitch (low RPM) setting and, if oil pressure is lost, the blades are moved to the high RPM position by centrifugal twisting force. (Some texts identify the high pitch and low pitch settings as coarse pitch and fine pitch.) Proper operation of the governing system depends on a supply of warm engine oil to the governor, which explains why you exercise the propeller during the pretakeoff runup — that action moves cold, thick oil out of the governor's oil lines and replaces it with warm oil from the engine sump.

To know what to expect in the event of engine failure in a single-engine airplane, then, you must know what happens to propeller pitch — one system goes to high RPM and the other goes to low RPM. In contrast, the system used by most manufacturers of propellers for multiengine airplanes uses engine sump oil to drive the propellers toward flat pitch, and engine failure

causes the blades to move toward the feathered position. The force opposing the oil pressure is either a charge of compressed dry air or nitrogen or a system of springs and counterweights. In gas-charged systems, loss of gas pressure means no feathering force. Exercising the propellers is part of the pretakeoff checklist for twins, of course, but there is an additional checklist item: the feathering check.

In the event of engine failure, the propeller blades must be rotated until they are edge-on to the direction of travel, to create minimum drag. When you move the prop control past the feather detent, governor oil pressure is released, and the air or nitrogen charge (or centrifugal force acting on the counterweights) forces the blade to the feathered position. The engine must work harder to rotate the propeller when the blades begin to move toward the 90-degree position, and this is reflected in increased manifold pressure. To prove that the feathering system works (without overloading the engine), pull the prop control back into the feather detent just long enough for the hum of rotation to change to a whop-whop-whop and move it smoothly forward again. It is much easier to do than it is to describe. If the propeller is sluggish and slow to move toward feather, scratch the trip; you never want to be airborne in a twin if you can't feather the prop on a sick engine.

"Wait a minute." I hope you are saying, "If loss of oil pressure causes the prop to feather, why doesn't it feather when I shut down the engine on the ramp?" Good question. There are internal centrifugal latches that keep the propeller from feathering when it spins down to 600-800 RPM, that's why. That's also why you can't wait forever to feather the propeller on a failed engine; if you let the RPM get low enough, you won't be able to feather the propeller at all.

The Piper Seminole (figure 3-3) is the only multiengine trainer in production as this is written, so most training takes place in "mature" airplanes. Many stalwart twin trainers are still turning out students after 40 years. I mention this because it is entirely possible that you will take your training in an airplane that doesn't use the prop governor system described above. Don't worry; study and understand the system you are using, and be ready to learn new systems as you move up in class.

Accumulators

As you read the emergency procedures section of the Pilot's Operating Handbook for the twin you are flying, you may find two unfeathering procedures, one for airplanes with an unfeathering accumulator and one for those without. Basically, an accumulator (figure 3-4) is a receptacle or tank in which oil is stored under pressure, to be released into the propeller hub when the prop control is moved out of the feather detent. It is a one-shot deal, so if the engine doesn't start on the first try, the procedure reverts to the no-accumulator method. The goal in unfeathering is to put oil pressure (from either the accumulator or the lubricating system) to work, twisting the blades toward a positive angle of attack. The Beechcraft Duchess book

Figure 3-3. Seminole

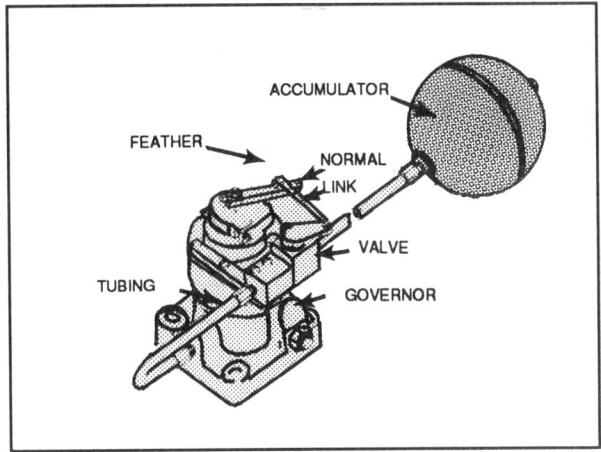

Figure 3-4. Unfeathering accumulator

calls for the prop control to be pushed full forward if accumulators are installed, and moved just forward of the feather detent if they are not.

Without an accumulator, you will have to get oil moving up to the prop governor by using the starter or by putting the airplane into a slight dive (or both) to get the blades windmilling. As the prop begins to move on its own, it rotates the engine and, via the accessory case, the oil pump. Oil pressure from the pump forces the blades toward their cruise position, spinning them faster and causing the oil pump to deliver greater pressure. Kind of a backwards process. Once the prop is spinning, all that is required is fuel and ignition, and you're back in business. It's similar to starting a stick-shift car by pushing it. Keep the power settings low on the recently revived engine until its temperatures have stabilized — you wouldn't want to run a marathon right after being brought back to life, would you? Neither would the engine.

Airstarts

Some airplanes simply won't start in the air without using the starter; no amount of diving will cause the blades to windmill. The Twin Otter is an excellent example. If you are training in such an airplane and the engine balks at restarting, you're on your way home with an engine out and its propeller feathered. Not good. Never feather an engine in training if there is any question about its ability to air start.

Air starts are hard on the engines, and the Beech Aircraft Corporation notes that numerous air starts without accumulators can shorten the life of engine mounts. You'll understand why when the engine vibrates excessively during an air start. Your instructor will probably have you air start an engine with its prop feathered only once during your training. It is not a skill you will need very often, because it is usually wiser to land at the nearest suitable airport and troubleshoot the problem. It doesn't help the engines to cycle between operating temperatures and cold iron, either.

Propeller Synchronizers

The subject of propeller synchronization will be introduced about one minute into your first multiengine takeoff and climb, when you or your instructor make the first power change. Unless the two propellers are rotating at exactly the same number of revolutions per minute (RPM), you will hear and feel a low-frequency throbbing sound caused by the difference in rotational speed. Set one prop (usually the right) to the desired RPM and then smoothly adjust the left prop control until the beat frequency between the two props gradually slows and then blends into a single tone. It will become second nature to you after a few power changes, or your instructor will go stark raving mad. Setting the friction lock on the power quadrant should keep things in tune between power changes.

When you move up into more sophisticated twins, you may encounter an automatic propeller synchronizer or synchrophaser. This device will keep the props in sync for you, but you must sync them manually before throwing the PROP SYNC switch. The automatic synchronizer system uses the right propeller as the master, and, if it senses a difference in speed between itself and the left prop, an error signal is sent to the left prop governor, driving it into agreement with the master.

Prop sync must be off for takeoff and landing and in the event of engine failure (if the right prop is spinning down to a stop, you don't want the left one to follow it, do you?).

Heat Consciousness

Excessive heat is your engine's enemy. In fact, it is the enemy of all of the hoses and wires crammed into the nacelle with the engine. If your twin's engines are normally aspirated, the heat developed will gradually decrease as you climb to altitude, in part because of decreasing ambient temperature and in part because the engine's power output decreases with altitude. Turbocharged engines operate at or near full power all the way to cruise altitude, so heat management is a real concern.

Your primary source of temperature information is the cylinder head temperature gauge. Oil temperature is a secondary indicator, because the oil carries heat away from the cylinder head. Increasing oil temperature is an early indicator of trouble, however.

You have three basic tools with which to control cylinder head temperatures: power reduction, cowl flaps, and mixture control. Pulling back the throttle means a change from your flight-planned airspeed, while opening the cowl flaps means added drag with some decrease in airspeed. Enriching the mixture exacts a dollar cost and eats into your fuel reserve. You must decide which method meets your needs, but you cannot ignore high cylinder head temperatures.

There are very few twins that are not equipped with exhaust gas temperature (EGT) gauges. These devices get their input from thermocouples exposed to the exhaust stream. Engine exhaust reaches its highest temperature when the fuel-air mixture is slightly richer than the best economy setting. Figure 3-5, from the Avco Lycoming Flyer, illustrates the relationships involved.

Although you should read the instructions for the EGT system for your particular airplane, the general rule is to set the desired percentage of power using handbook figures, and then lean until the EGT gauge reads its peak temperature

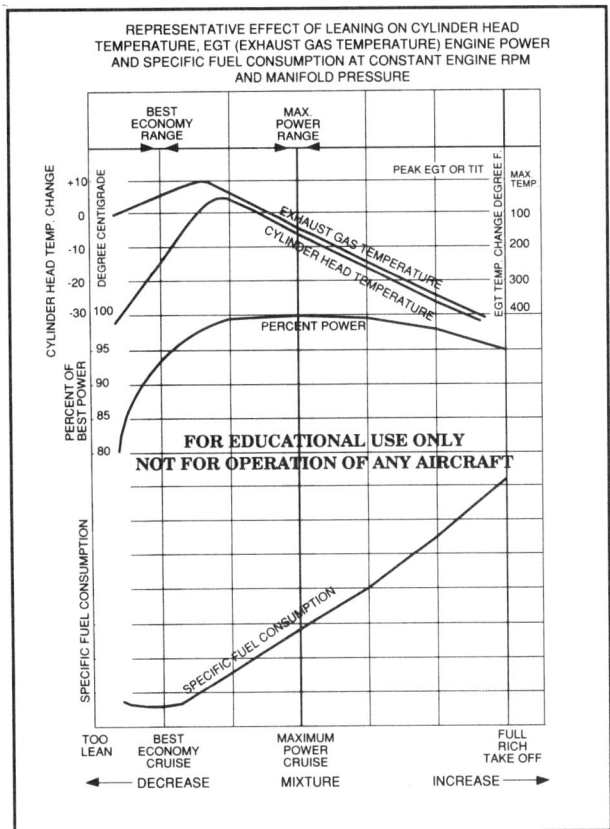

Figure 3-5. Leaning by exhaust gas temperature gauge

ence to the EGT, but you must do it intelligently, by the book. This is another area where what you do in one airplane does not necessarily apply in a different model.

The better EGT gauging systems have probes for each cylinder, allowing you to compare the exhaust temperatures. If one cylinder is running hotter than the others, the chances are that a clogged fuel injector is forcing that cylinder to operate on the lean side of peak. Single-probe installations rely on a probe in what the manufacturer has identified as the hottest cylinder, and the rest of the cylinders have to accept whatever you decide is best for the hot one.

Your multiengine trainer may very well have carbureted engines, just like your single-engine trainer, and in that case you already know the starting and operating procedures. On the other hand, this may be your first exposure to fuel injection, and a brief discussion of the differences is in order.

A Review of Fuel Injection

In the familiar carbureted engine, the fuel is drawn into the carburetor by the vacuum created by the downward movement of the pistons during the intake stroke, mixed with air in the carburetor, and distributed to the cylinders by the intake manifold. The temperature drop in the throat of the carburetor raises the hazard of carburetor ice, and the effectiveness of the fuel-air mixture delivery is a function of the intake plumbing. Getting equal charges into each of the cylinders is a difficult design problem.

(some systems will have a maximum temperature beyond which you will not lean, no matter what! Lycoming says that for almost all of its engines, 1,650 degrees F. is the limit). When you have noted the peak temperature, pushing the mixture control in until the temperature has dropped 50 degrees will put the engine at its best power setting. As you can see from the chart, the fuel consumption line slants upward as the EGT line slants downward — it is in your best interest to operate your engines on the hot side of the maximum power range.

Cooling the mixture by richening is called operating on the fuel side of peak. Some engines can be operated on the lean, or air side of peak, for best economy. Always observe the engine manufacturer's recommendations. The peak temperature limitation is based on metallurgical factors, because extended exposure to high temperatures will weaken portions of the exhaust system. You are hurting your engine's efficiency if you don't lean the mixture by refer-

A fuel-injected engine eliminates the uncertainty and imprecision in the delivery system by squirting precisely measured amounts of fuel into the intake of each cylinder. It obviously eliminates carburetor ice by virtue of the fact that there is no mixing of fuel and air in a restricted passage (throat) and thus no temperature drop. Figure 3-6 on the following page illustrates how the throttle controls airflow. Fuel is metered to the cylinders based on the pressure differential between the impact (intake) air and air pressure at the venturi.

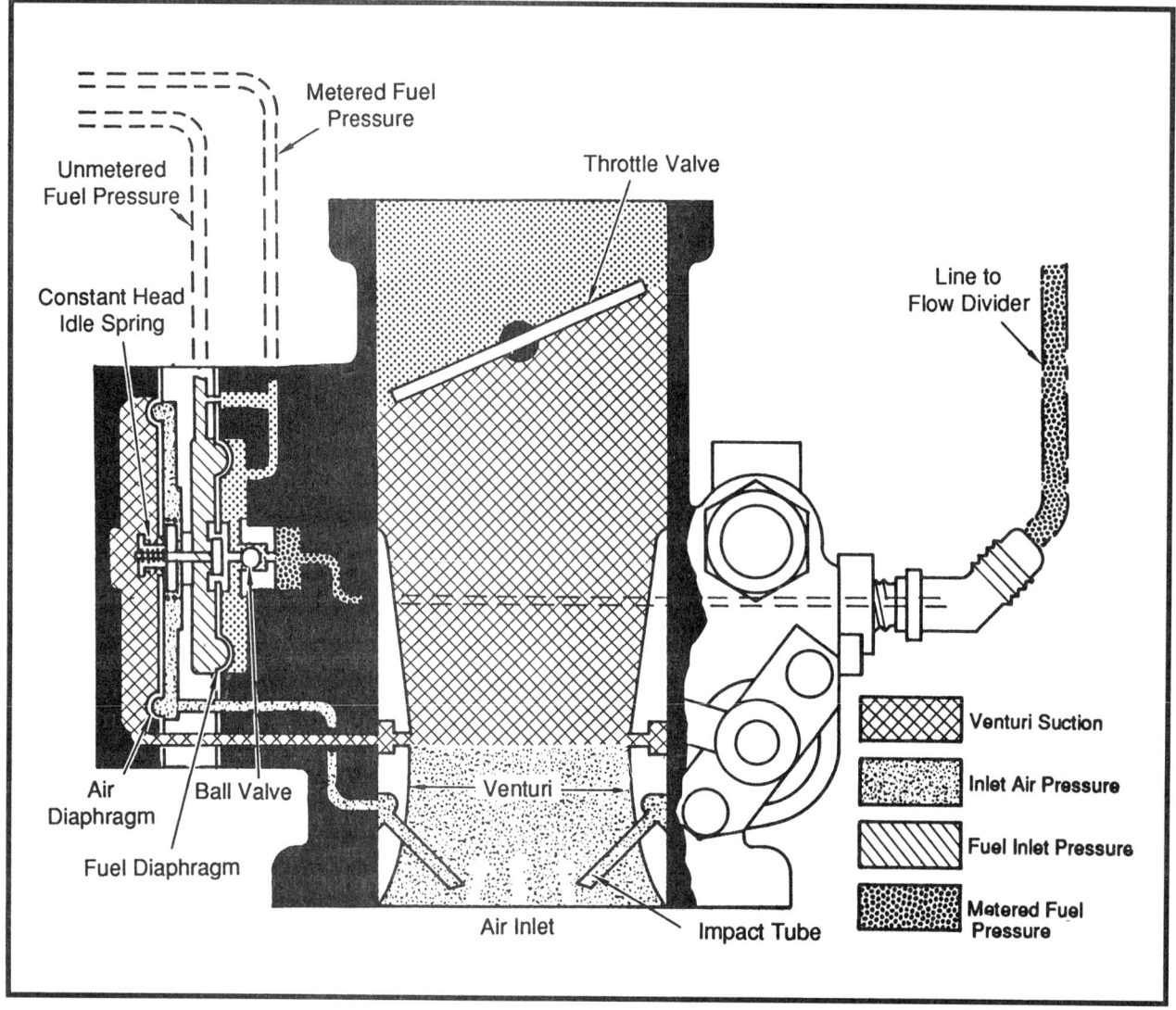

Figure 3-6.

Just because there is no temperature drop caused by cooling of a fuel-air mixture, don't assume that the danger of induction system icing is gone. An internal combustion engine must breathe air, and it will lose power if the flow of intake air is impeded in any way. The intake air filter can be clogged in many ways, and for the instrument pilot, wet snow is a frequent cause. No matter what the reason, if the manifold pressure begins to drop without any change in throttle position, your engine is gasping for air. Alternate air doors, either manual or automatic, allow air to be taken from inside the cowling, bypassing the filter. There may be a slight power loss when on alternate air, just as there is when you fly with full or partial carburetor heat.

A fuel injection system allows more precise control of fuel flow by providing a fuel flow gauge for each engine. These gauges are usually calibrated in gallons or pounds per hour, but they are really reading fuel pressure. An unexpected increase in fuel flow according to the gauge (above that called for by the handbook for a given power setting), is probably evidence of fuel injector fouling.

If you train for the multiengine rating in a typical light twin, it will probably have no induction ice protection at all. Few trainers are equipped to venture into anything more challenging than soft IFR, and their greatest protection against icing is most likely limited to carburetor heat.

MULTIENGINE AIRPLANE SYSTEMS

Figure 3-7. BE-55 fuel selector

Fuel Systems

If you are looking for an aircraft system which, if misunderstood, can cause real, life-threatening problems, look no farther than the fuel system. Systems vary from the simple on-off-crossfeed found in many modern twins, to systems with tank, pump, switch, and gauge combinations that defy understanding. A good example is shown in figure 3-7, the fuel selector of an older Beech Baron. (The label-maker placarding was mandated by an Airworthiness Directive.) As you can see, this airplane has a main tank and an auxiliary tank in each wing. However, there is only one fuel gauge on the instrument panel for each wing. A switch allows the pilot to select whether that gauge indicates the fuel remaining in the main tank or the auxiliary tank. Feed the engines from the mains with the gauges switched to the "auxiliary" position and you are in for a surprise. You can see the potential for problems

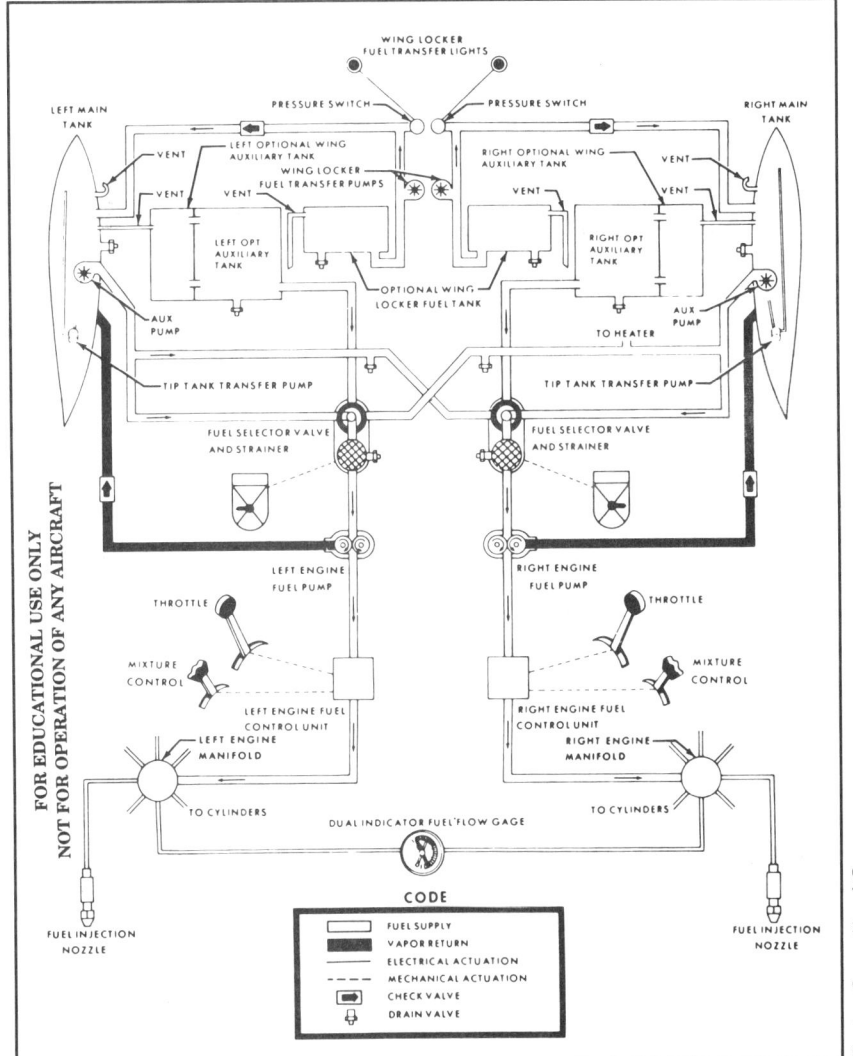

Figure 3-8. Cessna 310 fuel system

3-7

if the pilot has not studied the system and become familiar with its operation.

Figure 3-8 is the fuel system of an older Cessna 310. As you can see, the wing auxiliary tanks and the wing locker tanks are optional, meaning that they may or may not exist in a given airplane. Some 310s have both auxiliary tanks but only one wing locker tank. I mention this not to make you an expert on 310 fuel systems, but to point out the possibilities that exist when you move up into multiengine airplanes.

There will be a description of the fuel system in the owner's manual, but it won't answer questions such as "if the left tip tank transfer pump fails, will I be able to use fuel from the left wing locker tank?" That kind of answer must come from an instructor/pilot with encyclopedic knowledge of that airplane's systems or from a mechanic who works on that airplane.

Electrical Systems

When comparing the systems of a twin with those of a single-engine airplane, the distribution of electricity opens a whole new world of complexity.

One of the reasons that people buy and fly twins is the redundancy of systems, and an alternator on each side certainly meets that requirement. Instead of depending on a 60-amp alternator to feed juice to the radio stack, lights, and other systems, you will have two such devices. Twice as much available power! You can go down to the radio store and order one of everything — just be sure that the total electrical load you place on each alternator is no more than 80 percent of its rated output.

The Duchess electrical distribution system in figure 3-9 is typical. Just as is the case with your car's system, there is one "hot" wire from the alternator; the fuselage (or car body) completes the circuit. Follow the output of the left alternator with me. The little arrowhead symbol represents a diode, a device that will conduct electricity in only one direction. The loadmeter (amme-

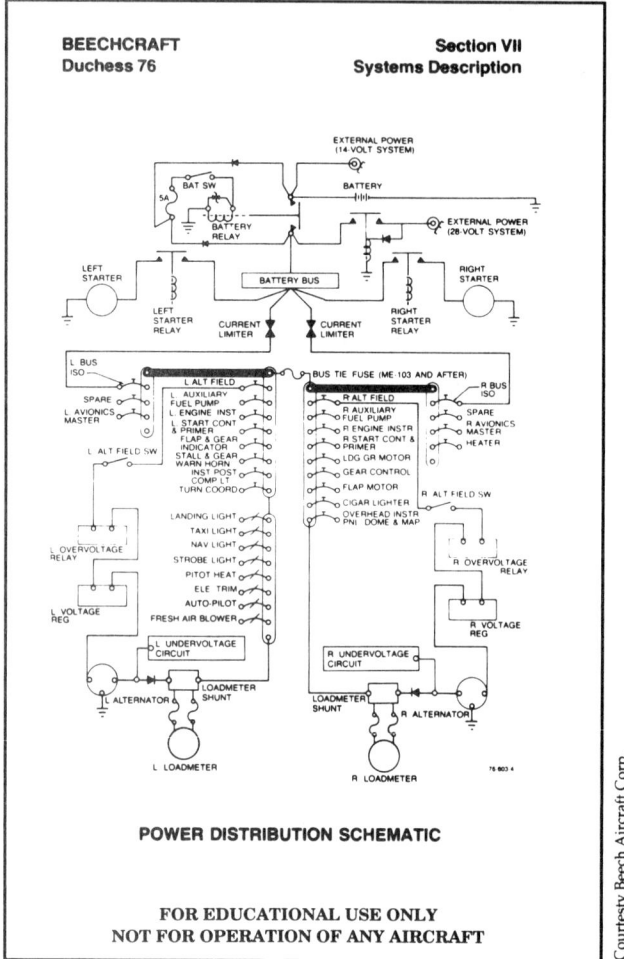

Figure 3-9. Duchess electrical system

ter) shunt is a part of the instrument on the panel which tells you how much current the alternator is supplying, so the electricity passes right through it. Follow the line up the page and you see what is called the left alternator bus. A bus is no more than a terminal board that allows the current from the alternator to be fed to hungry devices. The little arcs with slashes through them are combination circuit breaker/switches; you can tell from their labels that they are switches you would use frequently. Further up the page, the arcs have little tabs on their tops, representing circuit breakers that can be pulled manually; they protect devices that you do not turn off and on as a normal procedure.

The heavy black line at the top runs over to a circuit breaker called the left bus isolation breaker. It provides a means of disconnecting the left alternator from the battery, so that in the event of alternator failure the battery will not be discharged through it.

Follow the output of the right alternator in the same fashion, and you will see that power from each alternator goes to certain devices that are on its bus. The bus tie fuse, between the heavy black lines, connects the systems together and allows the left alternator to provide power to the landing gear motor (for example) if the right alternator fails.

Note that each bus has a circuit breaker labeled ALT FIELD and that current flows through that breaker, through the ALT FIELD SWITCH to the overvoltage relay and voltage regulator, and back to the alternator. Unlike a generator, an alternator requires field excitation before it can produce electricity. The voltage regulator controls the alternator output by controlling the field current. The OVERVOLTAGE and UNDERVOLTAGE devices warn you of these conditions through lights on the panel.

Assume that a single warning light has come on; you check the associated loadmeter and it reads zero. That alternator is out of business and the other one is carrying the entire electrical load. Your first action would be to turn off the alternator switch, even though you know the alternator is dead. Reason? Electrical problems can be intermittent, and the "failed" alternator might come back on the line unexpectedly. Your next action is to reduce the electrical load to a level which a single alternator can handle comfortably.

At this point, I would encourage you to make up a load-shedding schedule to be kept at hand in the cockpit. It should contain a list of just how many amperes each device draws, taken from placards or technical manuals, and a list of the essential items. For example, you may be able to get along with only one nav-comm and the transponder, without cabin or instrument lighting. Things that are heated by resistance (like your toaster) are power eaters. You may have to get along without your resistance-heated pitot tube and propeller de-ice if you are down to a

single alternator. If you keep too many devices turned on, the current drain of extending the gear may turn the cockpit into a black, silent hole. Think about those things.

Now assume a total electrical failure — follow through on the diagram. Obviously, there will be no ALTERNATOR OUT lights. The flashlight you always keep on a string around your neck (you do, don't you?) shows both loadmeters reading zero. First, turn off both alternator switches — you don't know which one caused the total failure. Next, turn the the battery switch OFF. Why let the energy in the battery leak away while you are troubleshooting? By turning off the battery, you are saving it for what may be a last-minute burst of juice to get the gear down. (Consider using the emergency extension system.) Pull both bus isolation circuit breakers; now one can't influence the other. Remove ALL electrical loads. Now turn on both alternator switches. Begin turning on essential items, pausing between each piece of equipment to see if it was the culprit that shut the system down. Watch the loadmeters; when you turn on the faulty device, the loadmeter reading will increase rapidly. Shut that device off again. Land as soon as practicable and have the electrical system checked.

Electrical systems can have some puzzling anomalies. For example, the continuous-duty fuel pumps in some Cessna 310 main tanks share a circuit breaker with the landing lights, so a problem in the light wiring can seriously affect your fuel management ability. If all of the electrically operated engine instruments are served by one circuit breaker, a fault in one in-

strument can wipe out the whole instrument cluster. Cultivate a friendly relationship with your mechanic; take him or her out to lunch and ask some "what if" questions.

Turbocharging

Ten years ago, a pilot moving up into a turbocharged multiengine airplane had a whole new power management system to become familiar with, because there were very few turbocharged singles. Today, you can rent airplanes with inflatable engines at almost every airport. I am going to assume that your first exposure to turbocharging will be in a twin, so here is a brief overview.

When you sip a soft drink through a straw, you are "aspirating" the fluid. Normally aspirated engines suck air into their intake manifolds. Pilots of airplanes with carbureted engines know that they run out of throttle at about 7,000 feet, because, although the descending pistons are doing their best to pull in a full load of air on the intake stroke, there's not much air available. Continuing the climb results in a gradual loss of power. This is about what would happen if some practical joker had poked holes in your straw — you would have trouble aspirating.

Complex airplanes, with fuel-injected engines and constant-speed propellers, evidence the gradual reduction in air density by losing about an inch of manifold pressure for every 1,000 feet of climb. Unless there is some means of pumping the cylinders full of air at sea-level pressure or better, a climb to altitude means a loss of engine power.

A turbocharger is that pump. Exhaust gases pass through the blades of a turbine as they exit the airplane, causing it to spin at high speed. A compressor, mounted on the same shaft as the turbine, compresses intake air and feeds it to the cylinders. The amount of "boost," or pressure above that available without turbocharging, is a function of compressor rotational speed and, because of the direct connection to the turbine, of turbine speed. Turbine speed is controlled, either manually or automatically, by a waste gate that controls the amount of exhaust diverted to the turbine blades. Figure 3-10 is a schematic diagram of a typical turbocharger system.

When the waste gate is fully open, the exhaust gases bypass the turbine, and the engine is essentially normally aspirated. The turbocharger is out of the picture. As the waste gate is closed, however, increasing amounts of exhaust gas go to the turbine blades, causing it to spin more rapidly. When the waste gate is fully closed, all exhaust gases pass through the turbine, and the maximum amount of boost is provided to the engine. The altitude at which the waste gate is fully closed is called the critical altitude. If you continue to climb above that altitude, the manifold pressure will gradually decrease. Don't look on that as a limitation: the critical altitude is usually in the mid to high teens, while service ceilings for turbocharged airplanes are in the upper twenties.

With a manual system (usually, but not always, an aftermarket add-on), you take off with the waste gate fully open and climb normally until the throttle is fully forward, then slowly close the waste gate while watching the manifold pressure gauge. The manufacturer's performance charts tell you what combinations of manifold pressure and propeller speed are approved at different altitudes.

As you descend into denser air, your first priority is to gradually open the waste gate until it is fully open, then use the throttle normally. Misuse of the manual control can result in overboosting, one of the worst errors of powerplant

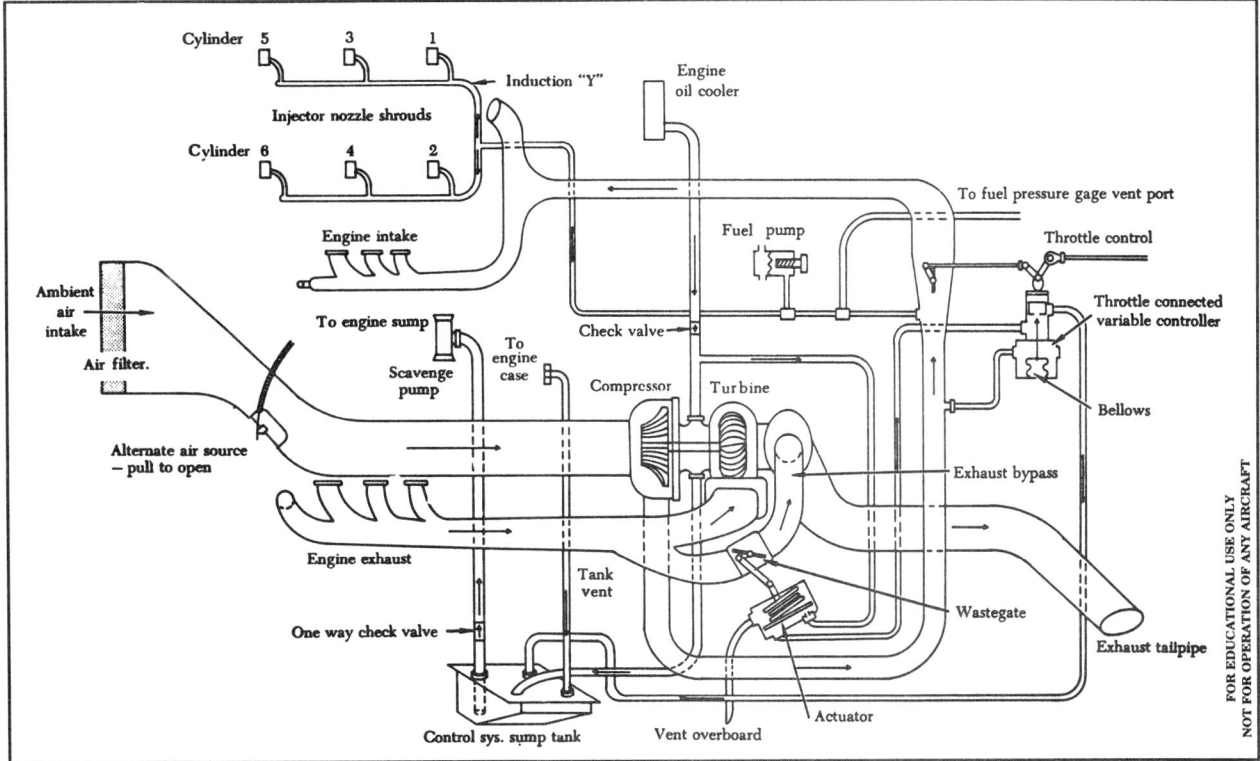

Figure 3-10.

management a pilot can commit. If the waste gate is left closed as the airplane descends, the compressor will pack the denser air into the cylinders at pressures they were not designed to withstand. You can imagine the effect on the engine of applying takeoff power with the waste gate closed. The engine manufacturer may require the engine to be torn down and inspected if it is overboosted.

Some cabin-class twins boast an automatic controller which senses changes in density altitude and adjusts the waste gate accordingly. Control systems vary too widely to be discussed here. Many include a fixed waste gate, which limits the amount of manifold pressure the compressor can deliver by allowing all exhaust gas over a preset value to bypass the turbine. These systems are mechanically simple, at the price of lower critical altitudes. More sophisticated systems react to density altitude, ram air pressure, throttle position, or mixture, and they require a lot of skill in adjusting the engine controls, while delivering more performance. Automatic systems are not foolproof, however.

A sticking waste gate can cause the same problems as a forgotten manual waste gate. You must monitor the manifold pressures at all times, but especially on takeoff — a stuck waste gate will cause the airplane to head for the runway lights just as quickly as will a failed engine.

Many pilots think that turbocharged engines are beefed up to handle the higher pressures. Not so. Consider a piston in a normally aspirated engine. On the intake stroke, it is pulled down by the crankshaft, creating a vacuum in the cylinder. No force is applied to the top of the piston. As the crankshaft continues to turn, the piston rises to compress the fuel-air mixture, causing increasing pressure on the top of the piston until — bang! — the mixture is ignited and the piston is forced downward in the power stroke. At the bottom of the power stroke, the piston reverses direction and moves upward to push the exhaust gases through an open valve. How's that for widely varying forces?

Now consider a piston in a turbocharged engine. On the intake stroke, it is pushed down by

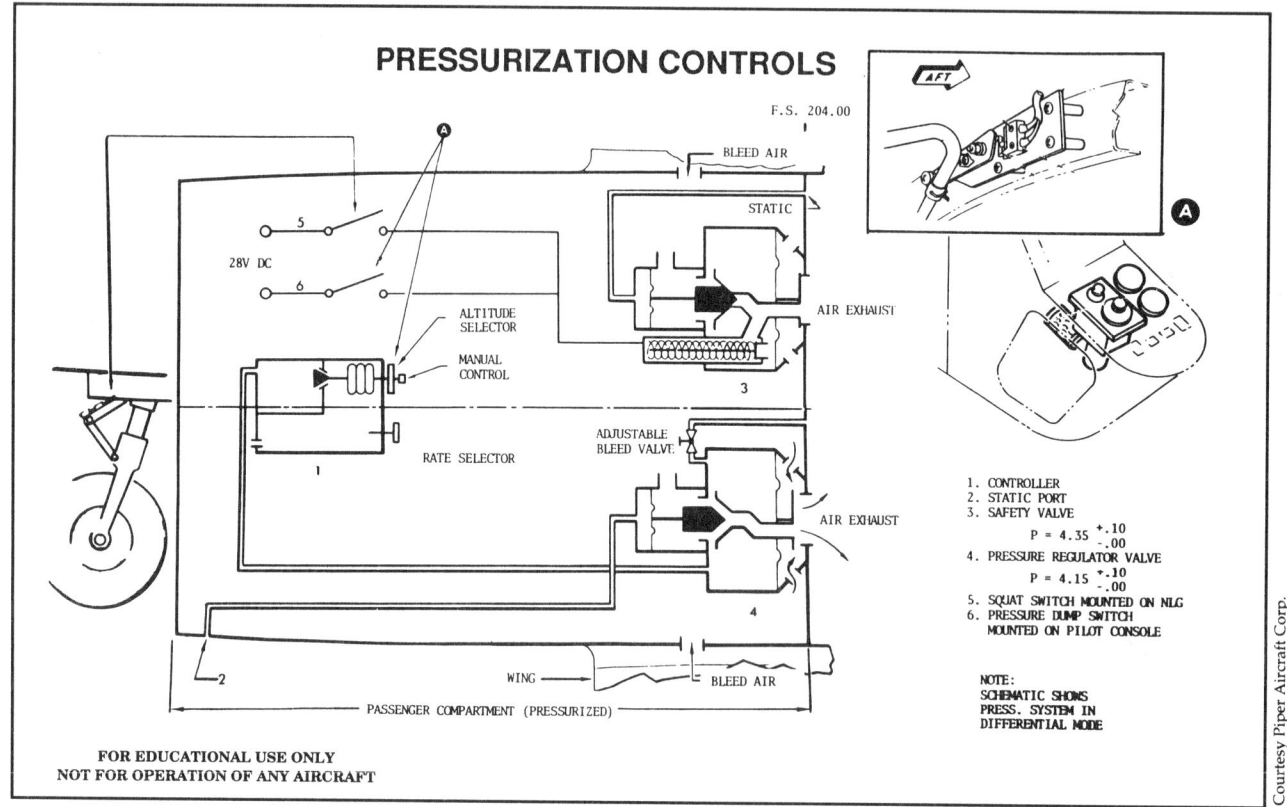

Figure 3-11. Typical pressurization system

pressure from the compressor. During the compression and power strokes, pressure is applied to the top of the piston, and on the exhaust stroke, the piston must force the gases through a waste gate and turbine wheel. Wouldn't you say that the pressures are more consistent in the turbocharged engine? That's why aftermarket blowers can be bolted onto aircraft — and automobile — engines. Of course, an engine and turbocharger combination designed to operate together will be more efficient and have fewer unexpected problems.

Heat Management

The real killer in the world of turbocharging is heat. The life of hoses and wires is shortened when they are baked. As the pilot of a turbocharged twin, you must be temperature conscious, balancing operational requirements against the need to keep the cylinder head temperatures within the normal range. The power output of a normally aspirated engine decreases as altitude increases, so heat generation during full power operation is limited to the initial climb. However, a turbocharged engine operates at nearly full power all the way to altitude, where the cooling ability of the air is diminished by reduced air density. The best source of cooling is a richer fuel mixture, so turbo'd engines are expensive to operate.

Many heavy twins are equipped with intercoolers — heat exchangers through which the compressed air must pass on its way from the turbocharger to the intake manifold. By lowering the temperature of the air entering the intake manifold, it reduces the amount of fuel needed for cooling. It fools the engine into thinking that it is flying on a cooler day, and when the temperature is colder than standard, you can get the same effective horsepower with lower power settings. In addition to the EGT, which measures the temperature of the gas passing through the turbine blades, intercooled engines may have instrumentation to measure the temperature of the air at the outlet of the intercooler. If you fly an airplane such as a turbocharged Twin Comanche, and can see the turbocharger in the left nacelle glowing white-hot at night, you will understand why chopping the throttle to begin a descent leads to metallurgical death for the turbocharger. If the ATC system allows you to plan a gradual descent, a reduction of two or three inches of manifold pressure every two minutes or so will allow more gradual cooling.

Pressurization

Turbochargers have the capacity to produce copious amounts of compressed air, and an excellent place to put excess air to work is in the cabin, as a pressurization system. The air will have to be cooled, of course, and some sort of safety valve must be provided to keep the airplane from inflating to the bursting point.

Those are the basics of a cabin pressurization system. The airframe must be designed to withstand the pressure differential that will exist when passengers can breathe normally at 25,000 feet while the outside air pressure is about 5.5 pounds per square inch. Two airplanes with similar powerplants may have differing operational ceilings, because their relative abilities to withstand internal pressures differ.

Systems to control cabin altitude vary widely, but they all have two things in common: an outflow valve and a safety valve. In figure 3-11, the Piper Aerostar system, the outflow valve is called the pressure regulator valve. The outflow valve provides the "leak" that keeps the cabin altitude at the desired level. Too much pressure and the valve opens, too little pressure and it closes. You control the desired pressure with panel controls. It's a good idea to set the cabin altitude below that at which the differential pressure will be at its maximum (or set the flight altitude on the pressurization controller higher than the actual cruise altitude). If you are flying at the exact altitude for which the controller is set, you will be "riding on the outflow valve," which will be opening and closing with every minor altitude change. This can be hard on passengers' ears. During climbs and descents, you may be able to control the rate of change in cabin pressure manually, or it may be controlled automatically.

The cabin safety valve is set to open at a pressure just a little less than the designed pressure differential, as you can tell from the ratings in figure 3-11. If the outflow valve sticks closed (have you been allowing your passengers to smoke?) and cabin pressure rises toward the danger point, the safety valve will open and save the day. None of this will do your passengers' ears any good, which is a good reason to (1) prohibit smoking or (2) service and clean the outflow valve regularly.

The cabin altitude should never be higher than the actual altitude. When descending, be sure that the cabin is descending more rapidly than the airplane. The airframe is not designed to handle a situation where the outside pressure is greater than the cabin pressure (even if the cabin didn't collapse, how would you open the door once you landed?) If the airplane is descending at 500 feet per minute, a cabin rate change of 700 to 800 feet per minute will hardly be noticed by your passengers. You should have the cabin at field elevation before landing. This is usually accomplished by setting the pressurization controller to an altitude 500 feet above the destination field elevation. That way, the pressure differential will be zero before landing. If you forget, a squat switch will dump the cabin pressure on touchdown, creating an uproar from the passengers that will almost make you forget your own aching eardrums.

Landing Gear Extension Systems

Very few twins have their wheels welded in place — the Twin Otter, Partenavia, (figure 3-12 on the following page) and Champion Lancer come immediately to mind. Most twins have fold-up landing gear, and you should become familiar with the system in the airplane you train in (you'll be asked about the gear system on the oral), then be sure to check the handbook on any other twin you fly. Gear retraction and emergency extension systems vary widely, even between airplane models from the same manufacturer.

The system most commonly used is electro-hydraulic — an electric motor operates a hydraulic pump, which provides the muscle. You must be sure that the hydraulic reservoir contains fluid during the preflight, and you should also place the location of the gear pump motor circuit breaker in your memory bank. The emergency extension procedure will probably require that you pull that circuit breaker before taking any further action. You don't want a sudden electrical glitch to turn on the motor when you are involved in pumping or cranking the gear down. Some electro-hydraulic systems allow you to hang out the gear by dumping the hydraulic pressure in an emergency; the Beech Duchess and Piper Seminole are good examples.

Does the system rely on hydraulic pressure to keep the wheels in their wells, or does it have mechanical uplocks? You'll find out by reading the POH on the airplane or by hearing the hydraulic pump run for a few seconds during the starting procedure. Gear doors and flaps have been know to sag a little when the airplane sits idle, and that quick burst of hydraulic pump operation puts them back where they belong. An electrical failure in a system without uplocks may result in the landing gear slowly extending itself when you don't particularly want it to.

The next most common method of extension is all-electric, and once again you should commit the location of circuit breakers to memory. The gear will only fail to extend at night, according to Murphy's Law, and you will have your hands full without trying to get your flashlight out of your flight case.

A gear system that relies solely on electrical power will be an additional concern if you lose an engine (and its associated alternator) or experience a total electrical failure and are living on the battery, because gear motors soak up prodigious amounts of juice. It might be wiser (again, depending on how other aircraft systems operate) to extend the gear manually and reserve the rapidly failing battery for other uses. With an all-electric system, if the motor jams you may be unable to extend the landing gear.

Figure 3-12. Partenavia

If you write Apache or Aztec in your logbook under "Model," the job of lowering the wheels is performed entirely by hydraulics, and, depending on the vintage of the airplane, there may be only one engine with a hydraulic pump — the left one. If this is the case and that engine should fail, count on doing a lot of hand pumping. If the engine is totally gone, be sure that the gear has fully retracted before you pull the prop control into the feather detent. That single pump is used to operate the flaps, too, in older Aztecs and Apaches, and if you operate the gear and flap levers simultaneously, both the gear and flaps will move with agonizing slowness. If a plumbing failure has left a puddle of red, sticky hydraulic fluid somewhere, there is a carbon dioxide "last chance" system to blow the gear down. When you pull the ring on the CO_2 bottle, the gas rushes into the gear extension plumbing and forces the gear into the down-and-locked position.

If your multiengine trainer is the first retractable you have ever flown, there is an idiosyncracy of fold-up airplanes you should be aware of: the gear down indicator lights may have already been dimmed to a feeble glow when you turn on the panel lights. This can be disconcerting if you are flying during daylight hours

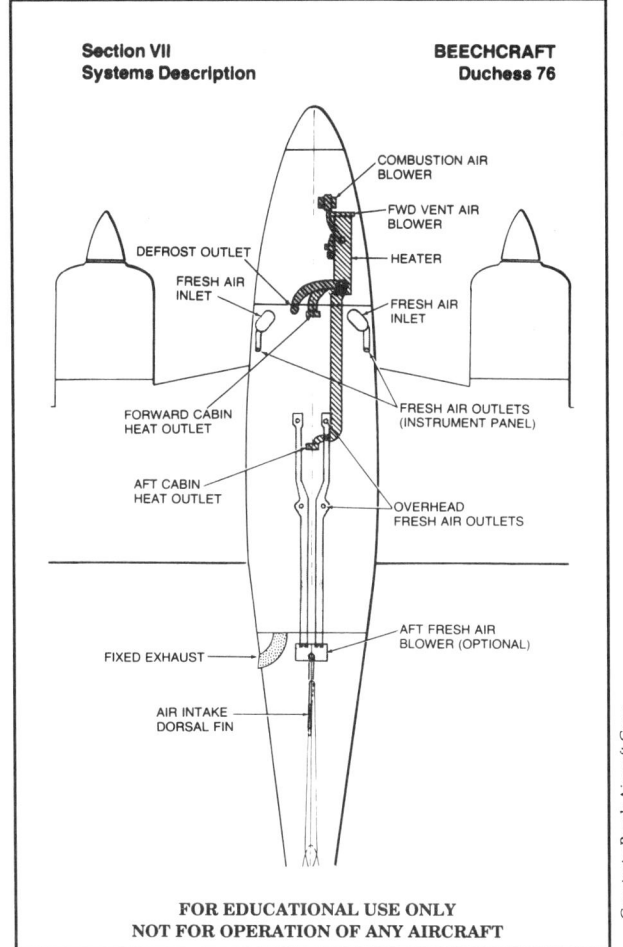

Figure 3-13. Duchess environmental system

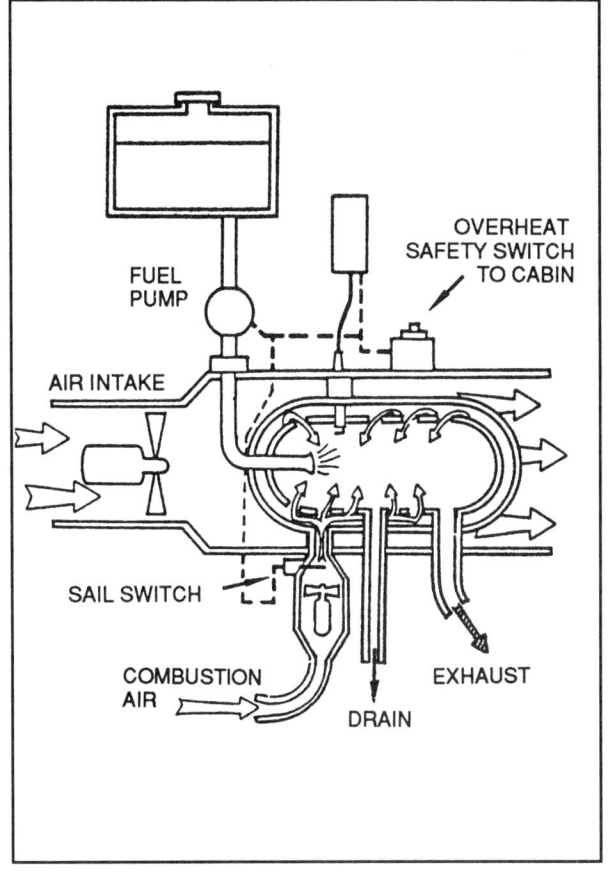

Figure 3-14. Typical combustion heater

and the last person to use the airplane left the panel lights on. Many a crash-fire-rescue truck has rolled toward the runway, lights flashing and siren blaring, because a pilot turned on the panel lights, extended the gear, and saw nothing when looking for "three green."

Environmental System

The environmental system in a multiengine airplane will demand more of your attention than the cabin heat and ventilation system in a single, because of the extended endurance of a twin. Four or more hours in an airplane without an operating heater will discourage the most enthusiastic light twin passenger. Single-engine airplanes get their cabin heat directly from the engine compartment, massaged and modified for comfort. In a single, a heater muff surrounds a portion of the exhaust system, and the red-hot exhaust heats the air in the muff. As long as the engine is operating, heat will be available (barring a problem in the ductwork). If you want or need another reason to get your multiengine rating, many carbon-monoxide-related accidents in single-engine airplanes have been traced to leaks between the exhaust system and the heated air being fed to the cabin.

Trying to move heat from a nacelle-mounted engine to the fuselage through ductwork without unacceptable losses is virtually impossible, so twins have gasoline-fired heaters located somewhere in the fuselage where you can't get at them in flight; the Duchess heater is in the nose compartment (figure 3-13). It works pretty much like any internal combustion device in that fuel and air are mixed in a tightly sealed chamber and ignited by a spark plug. Figure 3-14 represents a generic heater. The fuel comes from one of the tanks, combustion air is forced into the chamber by a fan, and the spark plug — well, it's a spark plug. Outside ventilating air passes around and over the firebox, is heated, and goes on its way to the cabin to warm you and your passengers. A thermostatic switch shuts off the fuel when the temperature reaches the comfort level that you have set.

It is a simple system, easy to use and hard to mess up. There are two major safety devices: the heater will shut off automatically if the supply of combustion air is interrupted or if the system reaches a preset maximum temperature. The overtemperature safety switch is located on the heater body where you can't get at it — if there is a malfunction and the breaker pops, you will have to land to reset it. The various blowers are protected by circuit breakers in the cockpit.

Combustion products are piped overboard. You can search out the location of the heater by looking for a short exhaust stack poking through the fuselage (with a dirty streak behind it). Nearby, you will find a little fuel drain tube that gets rid of unburned fuel. Make sure that it isn't bent or obstructed.

Which tank feeds the heater? If it's the right tank, and if you have shut down the right engine, do you really want to place the right fuel selector in the OFF position? If you crossfeed the right engine from the left tank, will the heater still work? If each wing has more than one tank, will the auxiliary or nacelle tank feed the heater? These are the types of questions you must ask yourself as you study the fuel and environmental systems. You must also include fuel for the heater in your preflight planning.

The heater not only contributes to the comfort of pilot and passengers, but it may also affect the accuracy of the air driven gyroscopic instruments. On many twins, the tiny gyroscopes that make the attitude and heading indicators work are powered by air from the passenger cabin, sucked over their paddle wheels by a vacuum pump. If cabin air falls below 40 degrees Fahrenheit, the gyros will not operate properly. Pressure systems, which blow rather than suck, do not use cabin air.

Vacuum System

From your first introduction to flight instruments as a student pilot, you have heard the attitude and heading indicators referred to as the vacuum instruments, and it's time to set the record straight. The pumps mounted on the accessory pads of your airplane engines are not necessarily vacuum pumps — they might be pressure pumps, depending on the airframe manufacturer. They might be dry pumps, self-lubricated by the graphite of which the pump vanes are manufactured, or wet pumps, lubricated by engine oil. As you scan the flight instruments, you may never know the difference.

Some mechanics feel that the service life of dry pumps is shorter than that of wet pumps, but all you need to know is that all such pumps have finite lives and that sooner or later you will lose a pump in flight. The nice thing about twins is that when it happens, you have a backup. Every twin has a shuttle valve in the line to the gyroscopic instruments from the pumps; when you start the right engine, the shuttle valve slides over to allow air (huffed or puffed) from its pump to operate the instruments, and when you start the left engine, the shuttle valve centers so that each pump does its little bit for the cause. When either an engine or its associated pump fails, the shuttle valve moves over so that the remaining pump can shoulder the entire load.

Question: what happens when the shuttle valve sticks and air from the good engine is blocked? The answer is that you don't have any motive power for the gyro instruments. Even two vacuum pumps can't beat Murphy's Law. Unless your Pilot's Operating Handbook is absolutely adamant about always starting a specific engine first, make a practice of alternating your engine starts. That will not only make any shuttle valve problems apparent, but will aid in detecting other impending failures that have been masked by the noise of the engine you habitually start first.

Each air-driven instrument incorporates its own air filter, and these are backed up by a central air filter. These filters should be changed at regular inspections, but may be overlooked. If you do much hard IFR flying, check the airframe logs to see how long it has been since the filters were replaced.

Ice Protection System

A few steps up the financial ladder, you might train in a Cessna 310, a Seneca, a Baron, or a similar light twin. Airplanes in that class are used for hard IFR and may even have some de-ice or anti-ice capability. Regardless of the type of airplane you train in, your goal is to move up into more sophisticated, more capable equipment, without stopping until you have a column in your log headed "turbine," so a discussion of ice protection is called for.

First, let's dispose of the certification requirements. Very few non-transport category airplanes are certificated for flight into known moderate or severe icing conditions. Your airplane may have boots on the wings, booted propellers, and a hot windshield, but there will still be a notice that "Flight into known icing conditions is prohibited" in the Approved Flight Manual. The equipment that is installed is intended to buy time to find an escape route, and should not give you a false sense of security. When you get into Part 135 Air Taxi operations, ice protection equipment and procedural requirements are quite stringent.

On normally aspirated and turbocharged twins, wing boots are pneumatically inflated to break off ice that is allowed to accumulate on the leading edges. Be sure you know where the inflation air is coming from. Two engines does mean two vacuum pumps, but if one of those engines quits, the remaining pump will be called on to both run the vacuum instruments and blow up the boots. If it is not up to the task, you will have one engine, no deicing boots, and no vacuum-driven gyro instruments.

Figure 3-15. De-iced C-414

Although it's best to follow the manufacturer's recommendations in every case, you should usually wait until one-quarter to one-half inch of ice has built up before you cycle the boots. Lesser accumulations will just flex rather than crack off as the boots inflate, leaving you worse off than you were before. When ice has spread past the rear edge of the boots to adhere to the metal surface of the wing, a "fence" of ice may remain when the boots shed their coating. This abrupt edge will catch even more ice, so watch for it; just a few moments in icing conditions can cause serious disruption of airflow over the wing. Wing boots require an extra measure of care during fueling. Conscientious line personnel will use rubber pads to avoid scarring the boots. A tiny hole in something that must be inflated in order to operate properly is bad news.

Structural ice will add drag to your airplane, and ice around the engine air intakes will reduce the amount of air available for the engine to breathe. Those factors alone mean decreased airspeed. Should you struggle along, accepting the lower speed, while attempting to maintain altitude? Absolutely not. You must sacrifice altitude to maintain a small angle of attack; if you increase angle of attack to maintain altitude, ice will begin to collect on the bottom of the wing. Some manufacturers dictate a minimum airspeed in icing to avoid this. Beech says 130 knots is minimum for Travel Airs and Barons, while 140 knots is minimum for other Beech twins.

The ice collection efficiency of a surface is inversely proportional to its radius. If the wing's leading edge has a four inch radius and a propeller blade has a radius of one-half inch, what looks like a trace of ice on the wing will mean a load of ice on the propeller. Hot props have electrically heated boots covering the inner one-third of the blade; the outer portions of the blades flex enough in normal operation to shed most ice, but you might have to cycle ice-laden props occasionally to hasten the process.

The usual hot prop arrangement is made up of two heating elements on each blade, with a timing device to apply power to the heating elements in a cyclic pattern. You can watch this action on the associated ammeter. If an inoperative heating element causes ice to be retained on one blade, you will experience severe vibration until it is thrown off. You will notice that many twins have plastic or metal shields on their fuselages in line with the propellers to reduce damage by ice slung from them.

When you compare the leading edges of the wing and the horizontal stabilizer, the difference in radius tells you that a little bit of ice on the leading edge of the wing means that considerably more is being collected by the horizontal stabilizer, back where you can't see it. Ice in that location may cause the tail feathers to stall when you are on short final (or in the landing flare). A good rule of thumb is that there is three times as much ice on the horizontal stabilizer as there is on the wing. Under those conditions, you become a test pilot; none of the numbers in the operating manual are valid when you are flying an iced-up airplane. The well-equipped Cessna 414 in figure 3-15 on the preceding page has boots on the propeller, wing, vertical fin and, although you can't see them, on the horizontal stabilizer.

An electrically heated windshield, or a heated panel that will keep a portion of the windshield ice-free, will avoid a situation where the airplane is clear of clouds, but you are still IFR in the cockpit. Do not delude yourself into thinking that heat from the defroster will melt a hole

Figure 3-16. External de-ice panel

in ice that you picked up at 15,000 feet when you attempt to land at an airport with a surface temperature below freezing. There's not enough heat available and too much surface to dissipate it. Pilots have landed by peeking out through the side windows, but it wasn't a pleasant experience. Many twins use an external electrically heated panel (see figure 3-16) on the pilot's side of the windshield. The heat radiated by this panel will provide a reasonable amount of visibility, although it shouldn't be expected to clear much more area than it covers — about 6 by 9 inches. These panels can be removed when there is no possibility of icing.

Electrically heated windows are a more expensive, but very effective, solution to the windshield ice problem. A grid of fine wire is embedded in the windshield itself, and when current flows through the grid, it clears the entire field of view. Never use electric windshield heat on the ground; without a considerable flow of air over the windshield surface to carry away the heat, the windshield may be softened. And if you are flying a pressurized airplane, you don't want anything bad to happen to the windshield.

You may find heated fuel vents on some airplanes. A vent clogged by ice means that fuel flow to the engine can stop, and collapse of the fuel tank or bladder is a possibility. A heated static port (or two) will keep structural ice from affecting the pitot-static instruments.

Emergency Exit System

An airplane with two wing-mounted engines differs from a single-engine airplane in another important respect: it must have an emergency exit. Some manufacturers provide window exits, some provide extra doors; few provide both. While you are giving your passengers the required preflight briefing on seatbelts, you might add a few words on how to get out of the aircraft if a sudden stop puts you temporarily out of commission. Before the briefing, though, be sure that you can find the exit; some of them are pretty well hidden by paint and putty (the Piper Seneca is a notable exception). A conscientious mechanic will not sign off a thorough annual inspection without exercising the emergency exits.

THE COMPLETE MULTIENGINE PILOT

CHAPTER FOUR

PLANNING AND PERFORMANCE

WEIGHT AND BALANCE CALCULATIONS

PREFLIGHT CALCULATION OF TAKEOFF WEIGHT and center of gravity location is essential for the safe operation of any airplane, but the consequences of failing to perform this simple task before launching into the sky in a twin can be disastrous.

The manufacturer's test pilot made sure that the center of gravity was within the design envelope before determining the speed at which directional control is lost when an engine fails, and, to get book performance, you can do no less.

There is more to the question of loading than a simple addition of weights to stay within a maximum gross weight figure. As you move from one model of multiengine airplane to another, or when you first sit beside a forest of knobs, you should calculate that airplane's power loading. That figure, the result of dividing the maximum gross weight by the total horsepower available, tells you how many pounds of airplane each horse must lift to make the airplane fly. A few years ago, the magazine BUSINESS AND COMMERCIAL AVIATION analyzed twin-engine fatal accident statistics and noted an increase in accidents when power loading exceeded 10 pounds per horsepower. For example, the Beechcraft Duchess manual lists a gross takeoff weight of 3,900 pounds to be hoisted on the shoulders of 360 horses, a burden of 10.8 pounds per steed. To stay on the right side of B & CA's statistical curve, Duchess pilots would have to limit their loads to less than 3,600 pounds. This is a calculation (and weight adjustment) that you can and should perform for any twin you fly.

Every graph in the takeoff distance and climb performance section of the Pilot's Operating Handbook includes weight as a variable, and you cannot predict your twin's performance without considering its effect. If the takeoff weight of your airplane and the density altitude combine to make the two-engine climb rate marginal, the climb rate will disappear on one engine. Limiting airplane weight is the only answer. Figure 4-1 is a graphic method of determining a safe takeoff weight. Although one of the reasons for moving up into twins is their weight-carrying ability, you might consider never taking off at maximum weight, especially at high density altitudes.

One final word on loading: leave some room for ice if the possibility of running into the cold stuff exists. If you are trundling along at cruise altitude and fly into the freezer compartment, structural ice will add weight to the airplane faster than fuel consumption can reduce it.

Any airplane will fly better, faster, and farther when lightly loaded than when grossed out, yet there is one plus to being heavily laden in a twin: a lower minimum control speed. That may seem odd, but these are the aerodynamic facts: banking toward the good engine causes the horizontal component of lift to offset the yawing tendency, and the magnitude of that component varies directly with weight. At light weights, you will have to bank a little further into the good engine to develop enough force to arrest the turning tendency or you will lose directional control at a higher airspeed.

Zero Fuel Weight

The term "zero-fuel weight" may be one you are unfamiliar with, if you are stepping up to twins from light single-engine airplanes. It is defined as the maximum weight of the airplane without any fuel in the wings. You will usually find this limitation in the form of a placard near the fuel selectors saying something like "All weight in excess of 3,600 pounds must be in the form of fuel." That makes 3,600 pounds the zero-fuel weight.

In flight, the weight of the fuselage is supported by the wings — there's nothing new about that. The wings must also support their own weight, of course, and almost all of that weight will be fuel at takeoff time. With the total weight divided between the wings and the fuselage, all is well. The problem comes when too much weight

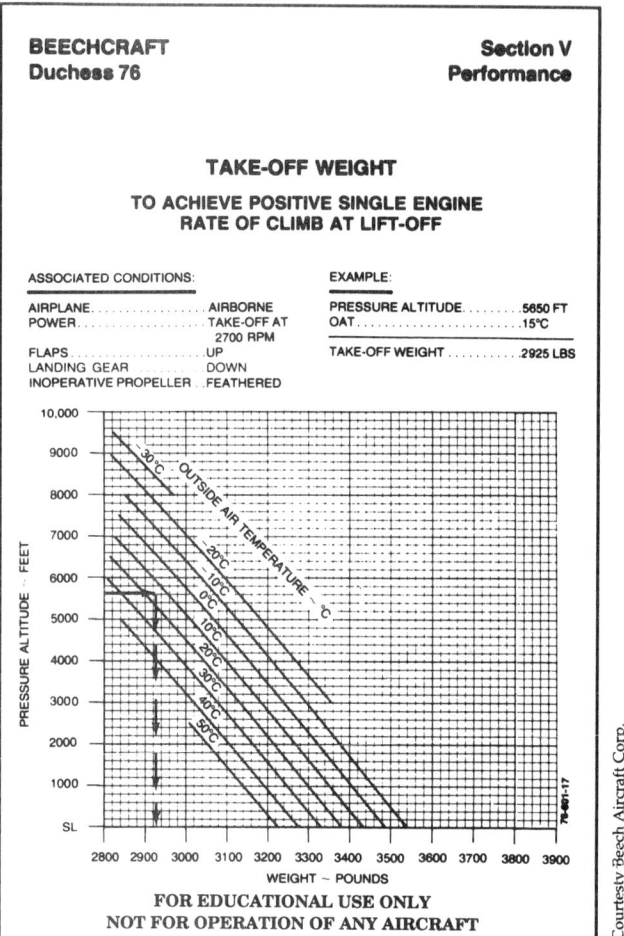

Figure 4-1. Safe take-off weight chart

is concentrated at the center of the spar, where the people and baggage usually congregate, and fuel burn reduces the weight in the wings. Under those conditions, if you have not observed the zero-fuel weight limitation, you are placing undue stress on the wing structure. Add a little turbulence to bounce the fuselage up and down on the center of the wing, and the result may be disastrous.

You have been calculating weight and balance since student pilot days, and the weight and balance solution should look familiar, except for the shape of the envelope. Figure 4-2, CG Range and Weight taken from the Seneca II manual, illustrates the typical shape of the operating envelope for a light twin. Note the zero fuel line and the line for maximum landing weight.

PLANNING AND PERFORMANCE

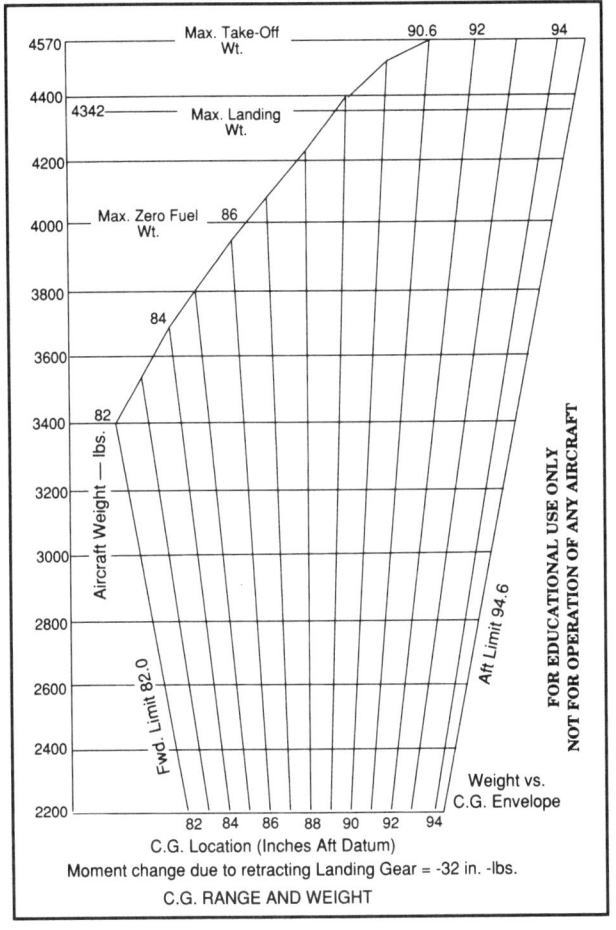

Figure 4-2. Seneca weight and CG envelope

moment from the airplane's manual, you will get these results:

Basic Empty Airplane Moment	272.2	pound-inches
Front Seat	32.5	pound-inches
Center Seat	29.5	pound-inches
Forward Baggage	1.1	pound-inches
Aft Baggage	8.1	pound-inches
Fuel	3.7	pound-inches
Total Moment	377.1	pound-inches

Dividing the total moment by the total weight in the time-honored manner results in a center of gravity location of .089339, which doesn't make much sense until you look back at the loading graph and note that the moments are given as moment/1,000. Push the decimal point three places to the right, and the center of gravity is a more reasonable 89.33 inches aft of datum.

Plot the intersection of 89 (can you find a pencil sharp enough to plot 89.33?) and 4,221 on figure 4-2 and you will see that the airplane is properly loaded, although it is loaded toward the for-

Let's try a sample problem to see how it works.

Basic Empty Weight	3,136 lbs
Pilot and Front Passenger	380 lbs
Passengers, Center Seats (forward facing)	250 lbs
Baggage Forward	50 lbs
Baggage Aft	45 lbs
Fuel	360 lbs
Total Weight	4,221 lbs

Piper supplies a plastic weight and balance plotter, which allows you to solve the problem graphically, but the pencil and paper or electronic calculator methods are always available. Using the weights listed above with figure 4-3, the loading graph, and getting the empty weight

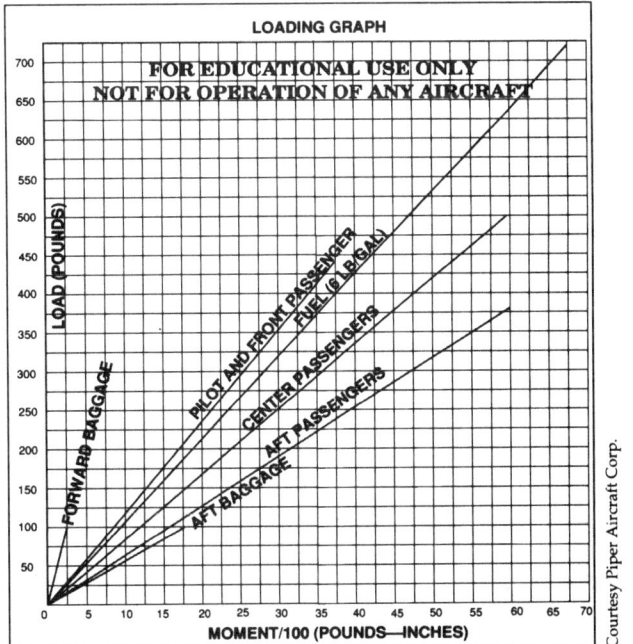

Figure 4-3. Seneca loading graph

4-3

ward center of gravity limit. I would move the forward baggage to the aft baggage compartment, if it would fit.

The Beechcraft Duchess weight and balance presentation makes you work a little harder, because the weight versus moment data is not presented graphically. Still, it will not challenge a $4.00 four-function calculator.

Our Duchess sample problem will be an instructional flight: student, instructor, and two loaded flight bags.

Basic Empty Weight	2545
Front Seat Passengers	375
Baggage	25
Fuel	600
Total Weight	3545

For moment numbers, look first to the Occupants list, figure 4-4. There is no listing for 375 pounds, but you can fake it by adding the moments for 200 and 175 (or any other combination that equals 375). In the column marked "Arm 104" (our Duchess is a later model), find a moment of 208 for the 200 pound pilot. There is no listing for 175, requiring interpolation. Add the moments for 170 and 180 and divide by two to get the moment for 175 pounds: 182. That makes the front seat moment 208 + 182 or 390.

The baggage listing, figure 4-5, has nothing for 25 pounds, so it's interpolation time again. A conservative number would be 42 inch/pounds. The fuel number from figure 4-6 is easy: 702. The moment for the empty airplane is listed in the Pilot's Operating Handbook as 2,775. Putting all those numbers together makes the total moment 3,951, and Beech has a tabulation of moment limits versus weight (figure 4-7) for you to use in determining whether the loading is safe or not. According to the table, at a weight of 3,550 pounds the forward moment limit is 3,850 and the aft limit is 4,171. The sample problem moment of 3,951 falls within these limits and you can safely launch on your cross-country flight.

OCCUPANTS

	FRONT SEATS			3RD AND 4TH SEATS	
	FWD POS.		*AFT POS.*	STD. BENCH	OPTIONAL
WEIGHT	††ARM **104	†ARM **105	ARM **112	ARM **142	ARM **144
			MOMENT/100		
120	125	126	134	170	173
130	135	137	146	185	187
140	146	147	157	199	202
150	156	158	168	213	216
160	166	168	179	227	230
170	177	179	190	241	245
180	187	189	202	256	259
190	198	200	213	270	274
200	208	210	224	284	288
210	218	220	235	298	302
220	228	231	246	312	317
230	239	241	258	327	331
240	250	252	269	341	346
250	260	262	280	355	360

† Effective ME-1 thru ME-20
†† Effective ME-21 and after
* Reclining seat with back in full-up position
** Values computed from a C.G. criterion based on a 170 pound male. Differences in physical characteristics can cause variation in center of gravity location.

FOR EDUCATIONAL USE ONLY NOT FOR OPERATION OF ANY AIRCRAFT

BEECHCRAFT Duchess 76
Section VI Wt & Bal/Equip List
USEFUL LOAD WEIGHTS AND MOMENTS
Courtesy Beech Aircraft Corp.

Figure 4-4. Duchess passenger loading

PLANNING AND PERFORMANCE

BEECHCRAFT Duchess 76
Section VI
Wt & Bal/Equip List

USEFUL LOAD WEIGHTS AND MOMENTS
BAGGAGE
ARM 167

WEIGHT	MOMENT—100
10	17
20	33
30	50
40	67
50	84
60	100
70	117
80	134
90	150
100	167
110	184
120	200
130	217
140	234
150	251
160	267
170	284
180	301
190	317
200	334

FOR EDUCATIONAL USE ONLY
NOT FOR OPERATION OF ANY AIRCRAFT

Figure 4-5.

BEECHCRAFT Duchess 76
Section VI
Wt & Bal/Equip List

USEFUL LOAD WEIGHTS AND MOMENTS
USABLE FUEL
ARM 117.0

GALLONS	WEIGHT LBS.	MOMENT—100
10	60	70
20	120	140
30	180	211
40	240	281
50	300	351
60	360	421
70	420	491
80	480	562
90	540	632
100	600	702

FOR EDUCATIONAL USE ONLY
NOT FOR OPERATION OF ANY AIRCRAFT

Figure 4-6.

BEECHCRAFT Duchess 76
Section VI
Wt & Bal/Equip List

MOMENT LIMITS vs WEIGHT

WEIGHT POUNDS	MOMENT/100 FWD LIMIT	MOMENT/100 AFT LIMIT	WEIGHT POUNDS	MOMENT/100 FWD LIMIT	MOMENT/100 AFT LIMIT
2300	2452	2703	3125	3331	3672
2325	2479	2732	3150	3358	3701
2350	2505	2761	3175	3385	3731
2375	2532	2791	3200	3411	3760
2400	2558	2820			
2425	2585	2849	3225	3438	3789
2450	2612	2879	3250	3465	3819
2475	2638	2908	3275	3496	3848
2500	2665	2938	3300	3528	3878
2525	2692	2967	3325	3560	3907
2550	2718	2996	3350	3592	3936
2575	2745	3026	3375	3624	3966
2600	2772	3055	3400	3656	3995
2625	2798	3084	3425	3688	4024
2650	2825	3114	3450	3720	4054
2675	2852	3143	3475	3753	4083
2700	2878	3173	3500	3785	4113
2725	2905	3202	3525	3817	4142
2750	2932	3231	3550	3850	4171
2775	2958	3261	3575	3882	4201
2800	2985	3290	3600	3915	4230
2825	3012	3319	3625	3948	4259
2850	3038	3349	3650	3981	4289
2875	3065	3378	3675	4014	4318
2900	3091	3408	3700	4047	4348
2925	3118	3437	3725	4080	4377
2950	3145	3466	3750	4113	4406
2975	3171	3496	3775	4146	4436
3000	3198	3525	3800	4179	4465
3025	3225	3554	3825	4213	4494
3050	3251	3584	3850	4246	4524
3075	3278	3613	3875	4280	4553
3100	3305	3643	3900	4313	4583

FOR EDUCATIONAL USE ONLY
NOT FOR OPERATION OF ANY AIRCRAFT

Figure 4-7.

Figure 4-8 on the following page makes it possible for you to plot the total weight and total moment on an envelope similar to the Seneca's; this gives you a better visual picture of where your loading lies in relation to the forward and aft CG limits.

Lateral Balance

As the pilot of a single-engine airplane, you manage your fuel consumption to avoid having one wing heavier than the other, and you will follow the same policy in a twin. However, the consequences of offcenter weight can be much greater in a twin if the engine on the heavy wing fails, because it will require more aileron deflection to raise the heavy wing and more rudder to offset both the drag of the windmilling propeller and the adverse aileron drag. Of course, if the engine opposite the heavy wing fails, the extra weight will help you control the situation. Unless your crystal ball can tell you which engine is vulnerable, you had better keep the load balanced from side to side.

Some fuel systems have within them the potential for a hazardous lateral imbalance situation. In these systems, the failure of a pump or valve may make it impossible for you to use fuel in one wing or to crossfeed it to the other wing. This may not seem too threatening at cruise altitude, but having one wing heavier than the other can really complicate a crosswind landing. If either engine should fail, you may have control problems on final approach. If a fuel transfer problem develops, the wisest course is to land at the nearest suitable airport before an imbalance can develop.

Performance Planning

Performance is what it is all about. When you move up into multiengine airplanes, you experience gains in climb performance, cruise speed, and load-carrying capability. However, those gains are only realized when both fans are turning. A twin with only half of its power available

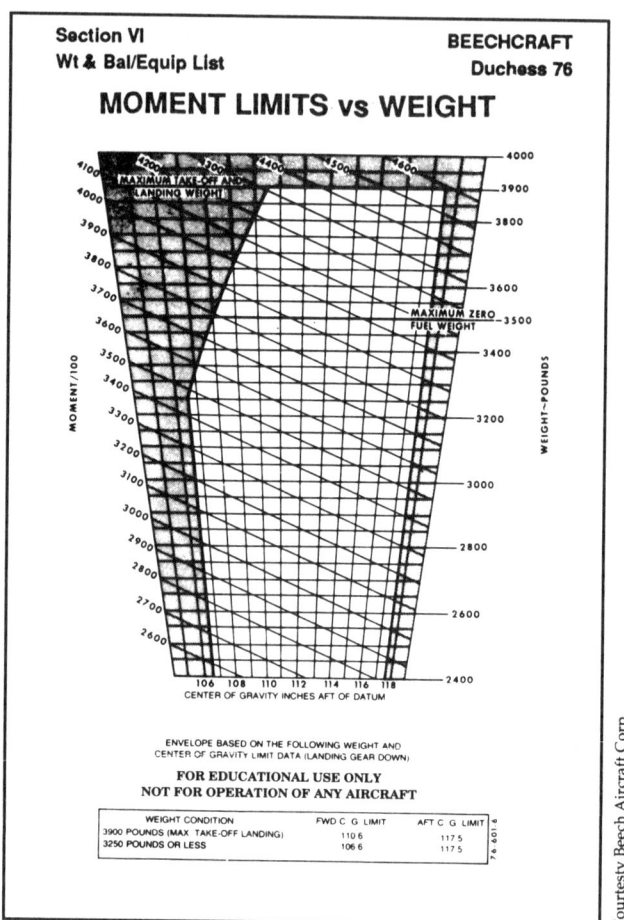

Figure 4-8. (above)

Figure 4-9. (below)

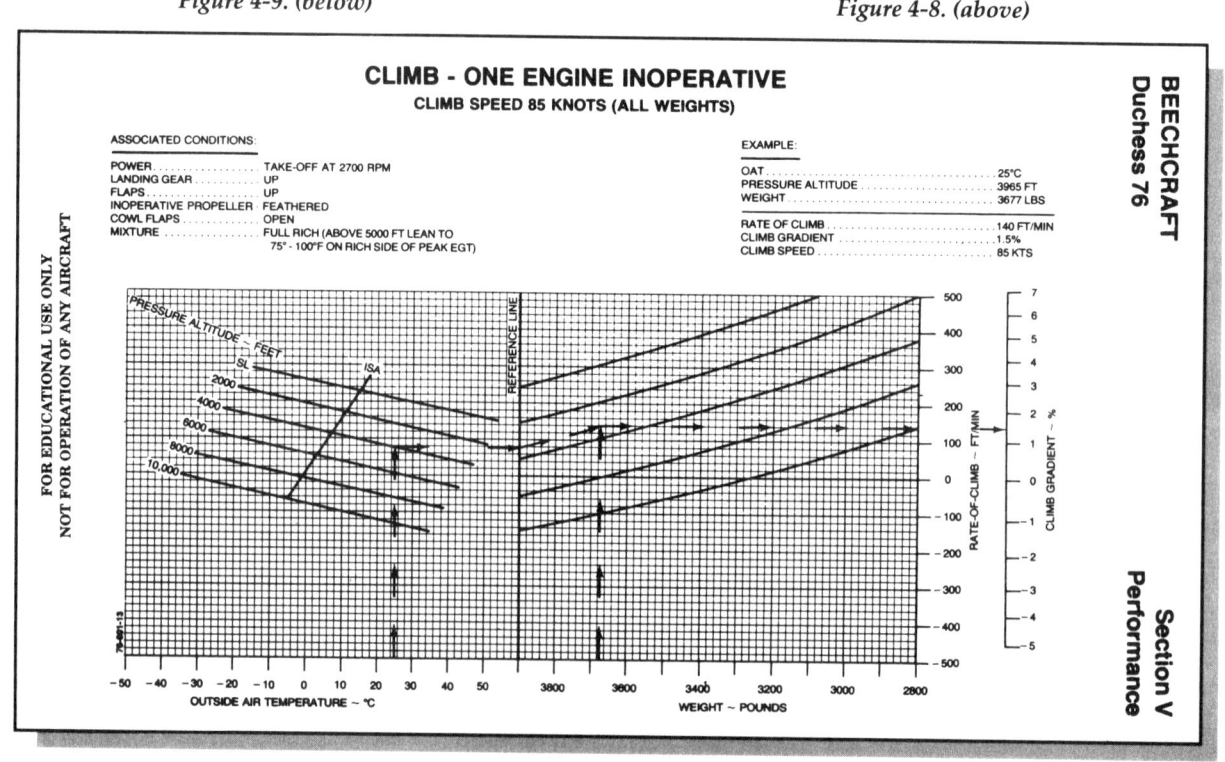

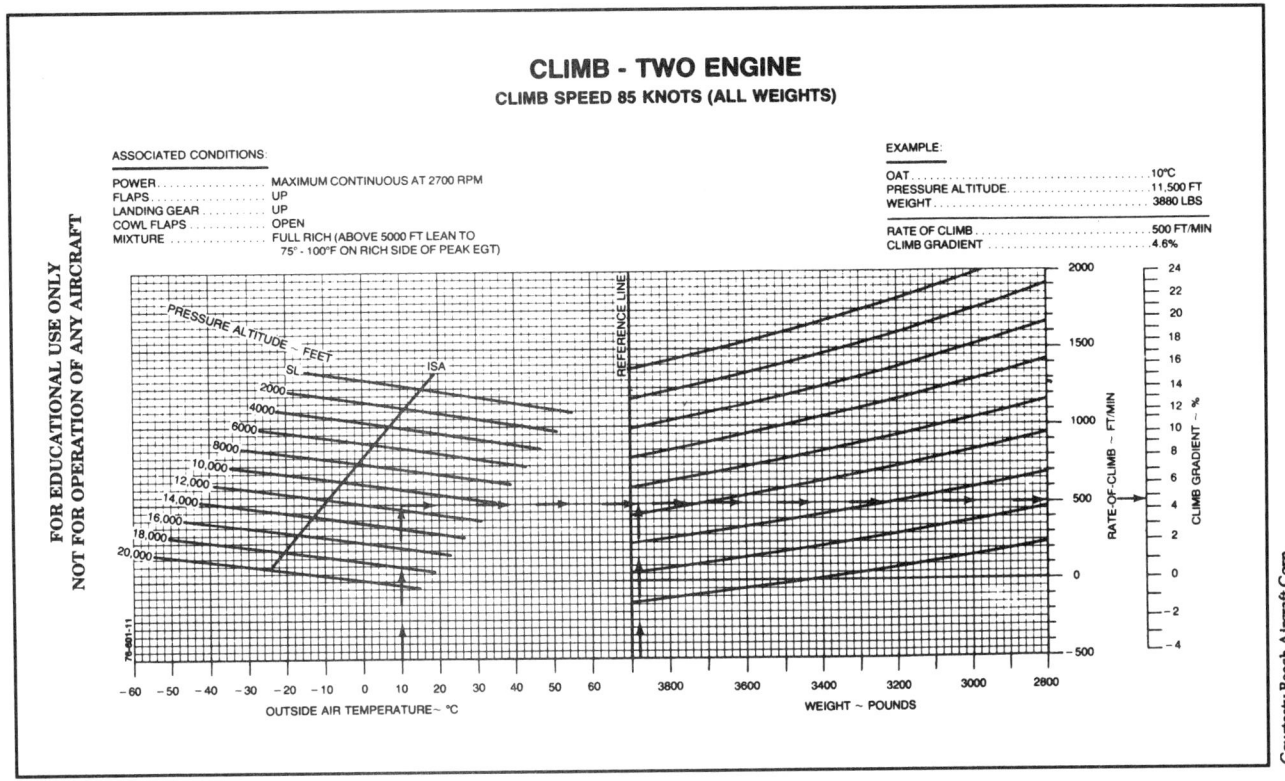

Figure 4-10.

loses out to a high-performance single in all categories. "Now just a darn minute," I can hear you saying, "are you trying to tell me that a Chieftain with only one of those 350-horse engines running can't outperform a turbocharged 210 with its 310 horsepower?" That's exactly what I am saying, and the reason is that although a twin loses fifty percent of its available power with an engine out, it loses eighty to ninety percent of its performance. Look back at figure 2-2 for confirmation.

The crippled twin's performance suffers dramatically for a variety of reasons. First, a portion of the lift developed by a wing with a nacelle-mounted engine is derived from the air being blown over it by the propeller. When that source of airflow not only disappears, but is replaced by turbulent airflow behind the windmilling propeller, you are worse off than you would be if there was only a single engine mounted on the airplane's centerline. When a failed engine's propeller is windmilling, lift over that portion of the wing directly behind the propeller disc is reduced considerably, and that wing's stall speed increases.

Second, a multiengine airplane both rolls and yaws when an engine fails, presenting more surface area to the relative wind and thereby increasing drag. Less power, less lift due to the reduction in airflow over the nacelle, more drag (until the offending propeller is feathered)— all of these elements erode performance. The immediate actions required by the manufacturer's engine-out checklist are designed to restore as much lift as possible, decrease drag, and add whatever power is needed for you to maintain control of the airplane's attitude.

The purpose of an airplane engine is to pull the wing forward through the air (the fuselage goes along for the ride); think of the engine as an air pump, in which air is mixed with fuel, set on fire, and pumped overboard. In the process, every power stroke contributes its energy toward rotating the propeller. When the fire goes out, however, the propeller blades are rotated by the airplane's forward motion and the action is reversed; the propeller drives the pistons up and down in their cylinders against the pressure of the air trapped in them plus the load of all the accessories. This is why the windmilling propeller creates drag, acting almost as a flat circular plate with a diameter equal to that of the propeller disc. To eliminate that flat-plate drag, the windmilling propeller must be stopped by rotating its blades to the feathered position.

Graphs from the Pilot's Operating Handbook will help explain the loss of climb performance with an engine feathered. Using figures 4-9 and 4-10 on the previous pages, you can readily compare the two engine climb rate with the single-engine climb rate under the same conditions.

OAT	+ 20 C.
Pressure altitude	2,000 feet
Weight	3,600 pounds

If you haven't used this kind of performance graph before, it might be a good idea to run through a problem. You will see a lot of these graphs in twin manuals. If you were preparing for an FAA written examination, I would suggest that you equip yourself with a transparent overlay, a pair of dividers, and several sharp pencils. Because you are not preparing for any kind of examination except the very practical test of not having enough runway or performance to take off safely, a practical approach is in order.

The first step is to enter density altitude, which is a combination of temperature and pressure altitude. Find the +20 number along the baseline and follow the vertical line upward to its intersection with the 2,000-foot pressure altitude line; that combination defines the density altitude. Draw a horizontal line over to the reference line or do it my way — the density altitude point is just over 18 squares down from the top.

Here's where your keen eye and sense of proportion come into play. Draw or eyeball a line that closely parallels one of the upward slanting lines in the weight area until it intersects with a

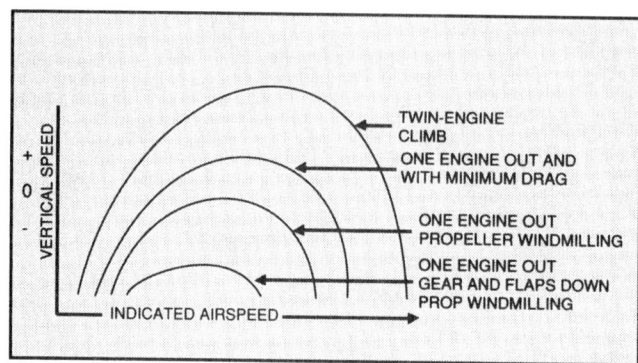

Figure 4-11. Configurations vs vertical speed

vertical line drawn up from 3,600 pounds. Now draw a straight horizontal line from that point to the right margin to determine the rate of climb.

A sharp eye and a sharp pencil working together make the climb rate with both engines running about 1,300 feet per minute. Now apply those same conditions to the second graph, the climb with one engine inoperative. The sharpest eye and pencil can't improve on a climb rate of 200 feet per minute, only 15 percent of the two-engine climb rate. When one of the engines fails, 85 percent of the climb performance disappears.

To get even this meager amount of performance, it is essential that you reduce drag to a minimum; by applying full power to the good engine, you have done as much as you can on the thrust side of the equation. The landing gear and flaps are obvious drag items, and the windmilling propeller must be feathered to eliminate its drag. With the airplane under control, banking so that the ball is deflected one-half ball width toward the good engine will establish zero sideslip and eliminate the drag caused by slipping toward the dead engine — one ball width while gaining control, one-half ball width for best performance after you are in charge again.

Figure 4-11 shows how the drag items listed above affect vertical speed.

Airspeed control is essential if you expect to get book performance from your multiengine airplane, and you must know the appropriate airspeed for each condition of flight. Some of the airspeed designations will be familiar from your earlier training, while others will be unique to multiengine flight. Your multiengine examiner will ask you to recite the V-speeds and explain them. The following sections discuss the speeds you should know.

Minimum Controllable Airspeed

The red line on the airspeed indicator is Vmc, minimum-controllable airspeed, and it will be mentioned more than once in this book. The manufacturer, complying with conditions specified by the FAA (Part 23), has determined that any attempt to take off and climb at a speed slower than Vmc with one engine inoperative and its propeller windmilling will result in loss of directional control. You should respect the red line as a minimum airspeed, and understand that as airspeed is reduced toward Vmc, your ability to control the aircraft is deteriorating. It's not an on-off, yes-no situation—if Vmc is 80 knots, you will still have a tiger by the tail at 82 knots with an engine out (meaning lots of rudder). As airspeed increases above the red line, controllability will improve, but you will still have a sick bird on your hands.

I was careful to say that the manufacturer determined Vmc under certain conditions set forth in FAR 23. Let's examine each of those conditions to see how it affects Vmc.

"Takeoff or maximum-available power on the engines."

The greatest yawing and rolling forces are created when one engine is developing maximum power and the other is suddenly made inoperative. An airplane engine and propeller combination develop maximum-rated horsepower at sea level; as density altitude is increased by higher pressure altitude or temperature, the power output decreases and the rolling and yawing forces are reduced. A greater angle of attack

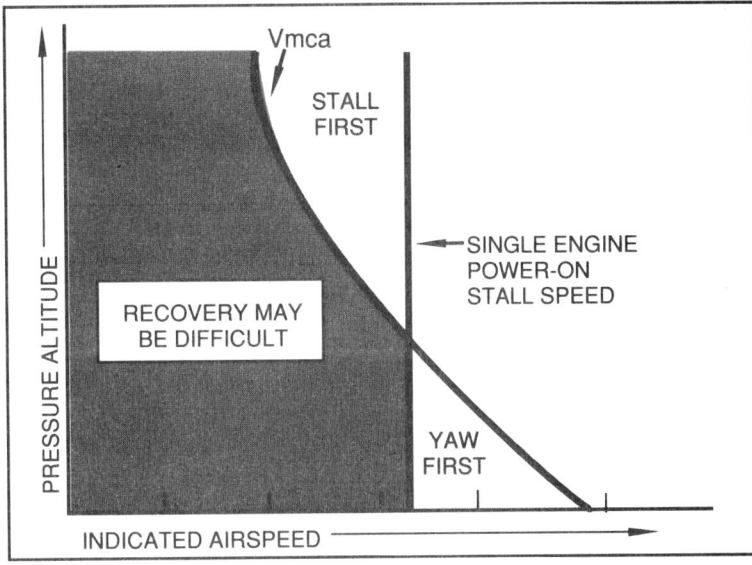

Figure 4-12. Stall speed, Vmc and altitude

(lower airspeed) is then required for those forces to become great enough to endanger your ability to control the airplane. Figure 4-12 illustrates how Vmc decreases as density altitude increases. Note that the indicated airspeed at which the airplane will stall stays constant as altitude changes, and that at some altitude, Vmc and stall speed will coincide. If an engine fails at a higher altitude, with an indicated airspeed near the power-on stall speed (a most unlikely situation), the airplane may enter a spin. It is safe to say that your airspeed needle should never be below the red line except during the landing flare. (Those few airplanes that require liftoff speeds at or near Vmc are discussed elsewhere.)

"The most unfavorable center of gravity."

All three axes of control — pitch, roll, and yaw — act through the center of gravity (CG). If the CG is at or near the most rearward limit, the distance between the CG and the rudder is reduced, which reduces the amount of yawing leverage the rudder can exert. This means that your ability to control the airplane in an emergency is improved as the center of gravity is moved forward.

Part 23 does not address the question of lateral movement of the center of gravity, but a lateral imbalance might cause a lot of grief. You are already aware of the need to keep wing tank

fuel in balance from your experience in single-engine airplanes, so nothing further needs to be said about fuel management. However, multiengine airplanes that have wing lockers require special consideration in weight distribution. What happens if you put the tennis balls and racquets in the right wing locker, and load the golf clubs and the rest of the recreational equipment in the left wing locker, and the left engine fails? Supervise the loading of the wing lockers to be sure the weight is equally distributed.

"The maximum sea level takeoff weight (or any lesser weight necessary to show Vmc)."

Minimum controllable airspeed increases as weight is reduced, for reasons discussed later in this chapter. This is the only performance factor that is affected adversely by weight reduction.

"Flaps in the takeoff position."

The intent is to simulate, as closely as possible, the situation that would exist just after liftoff, at the beginning of the initial climb segment.

"Landing gear retracted."

The same scenario as for the flap setting.

"The propeller of the inoperative engine windmilling."

This is to create the most drag and the largest yawing moment for the Vmc certification tests. Feathering the offending propeller eliminates the drag and improves controllability.

"The airplane airborne and ground effect negligible."

This requirement adds to the realism of the "just after takeoff" situation.

Minimum Safe Single-Engine Speed

The General Aviation Manufacturer's Association, following Beechcraft's lead, responded to a rash of multiengine training accidents by suggesting that instructors observe a new V-speed, Vsse. This is the minimum speed for intentional engine failures, and it is usually 5 or 6 knots above Vmc. Your instructor should know Vsse for your airplane. Vsse allows a comfortable margin above Vmc, yet it is slow enough to give you a workout. If your instructor insists on practicing low-altitude engine failures at red line airspeed, get another instructor.

Best Angle and Best Rate-of-Climb Speeds

The definitions of best angle-of-climb and best rate-of-climb speed do not change when you sit between two engines instead of behind one, and their designations (Vx and Vy) don't change either. These speeds are not marked on the airspeed indicator. Despite the emphasis that I must place on engine-out emergencies, in my opinion you should determine and use the two-engine performance speeds. The slight cushion that they provide will prove invaluable during the critical first few seconds if something does go awry.

Landing Gear Extension and Operating Speeds

Most single-engine retractables have a single gear speed, which applies both to extension of the gear and operations with the gear down. Many twins have two gear speeds: Vlo, which governs the speed at which you can operate the gear, and Vle, which limits the speed at which you can fly with it extended. If gear doors must open to let the wheels hang out and then close again to cover the wheel well, Vlo will probably be slower to keep the gear doors from blowing

PLANNING AND PERFORMANCE

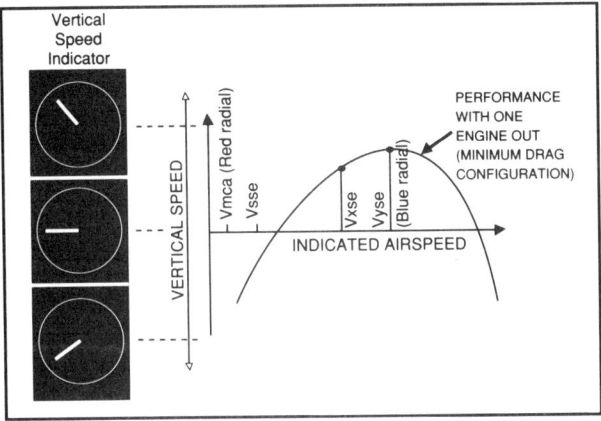

Figure 4-13.

away during the extension cycle. For those airplanes with nose gears that move forward during the retraction cycle, you may note a second Vlo speed: the maximum speed at which the gear should be retracted.

Engine-Out Climb Speeds

The Approved Flight Manual or Pilot's Operating Handbook (depending on the age of the airplane) will list the speeds to be maintained in the event of an engine failure. The single-engine best angle-of-climb speed (Vxse) is of marginal importance, in my opinion. The operating manual says that you should use the best angle speed until any obstacles have been cleared, and then accelerate to the best rate-of-climb speed. Believe me, if there is an obstacle in the takeoff path high enough to worry you, considering the weight of the airplane and the density altitude, it would be wiser to choose another path than to plan on maintaining Vxse until you clear the obstacle. Don't bet your life that you and your airplane can deliver book performance under actual conditions.

The best single-engine rate-of-climb speed (Vyse) is marked on the airspeed indicator by a blue radial line, and is usually called "blue line speed." According to the FAA's Flight Training Handbook (AC 61-21A), this is your target speed if an engine fails just after takeoff. Figure 4-13 illustrates that rate of climb will decrease at airspeeds higher or lower than Vyse. Many instructors (myself included) recommend that you use the all-engine best rate of climb speed (Vy) as a target, reasoning that you will lose a few knots while you are reacting to an engine failure. The FAA says to use the blue line speed, period. Work it out with your instructor.

There is nothing to be gained by accelerating beyond Vy until you have attained a safe maneuvering altitude. In the early stages of a multiengine takeoff, altitude is far more important than airspeed. Figure 4-14 illustrates why you shouldn't lower the nose and accelerate to cruise-climb airspeed too soon: drag increases as the square of the airspeed, and the power required to maintain that airspeed increases as the cube of the airspeed. You don't want to add drag by accelerating while the possibility exists that you might lose half of the thrust while close to the ground. The graph also explains why no dramatic performance increase is gained by retracting the gear early; if airspeed is held constant during the initial climb, the drag of the extended gear also remains constant. Retracting the rollers while there is still usable pavement ahead is foolhardy.

Maneuvering Speed, Normal Operating Speed and Never-Exceed Speed

The meanings of Va, Vno, and Vne are the same in a twin as they are in a single-engine airplane. However, the fact that two engines make high speeds possible and weather penetration less formidable cause some multiengine pilots to

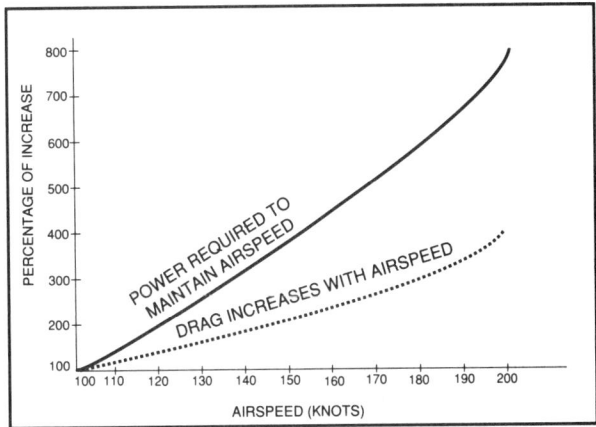

Figure 4-14. Drag vs airspeed

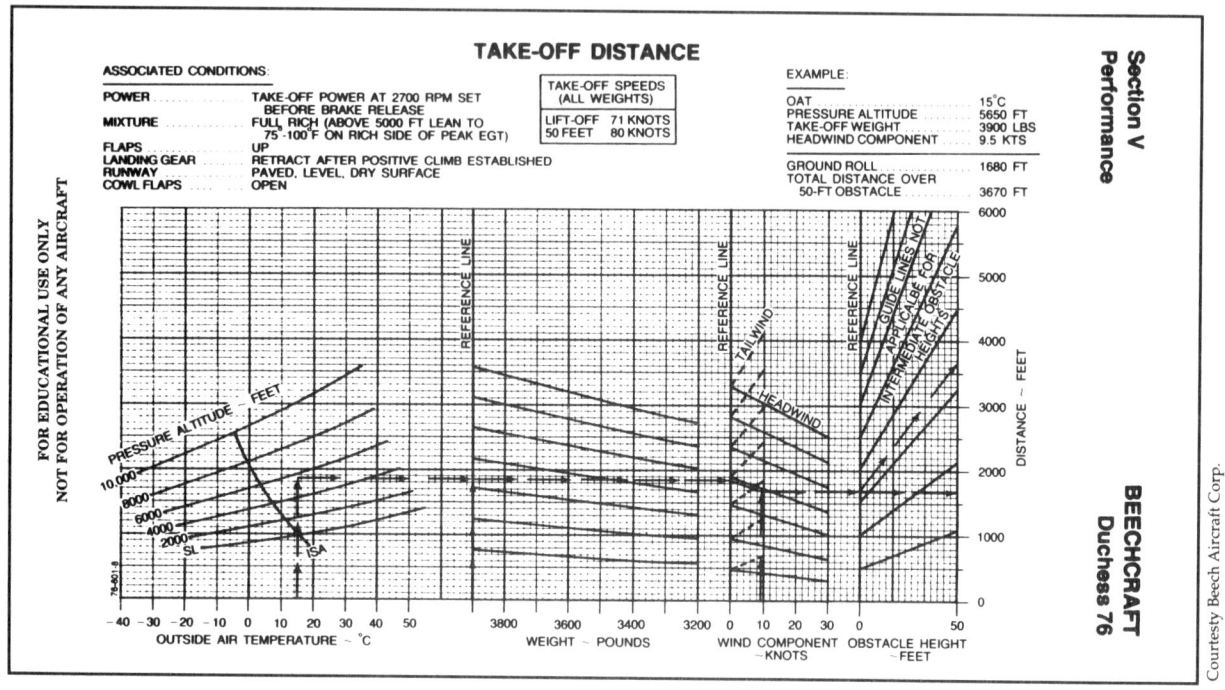

Figure 4-16. Duchess takeoff distance chart

take chances that they would not take in a single. Don't do it. The aerodynamic forces that cause inflight structural failure are not dependent on the number of engines.

Performance Airspeeds Versus Weight

When the aerodynamicists and engineers go over the data from test flights of new airplanes, they reduce all of the numbers to reflect what would happen to that airplane at maximum gross weight at sea level on a standard day. Those are the numbers that appear in the Pilot's Operating Handbook and are, in the case of Vmc and Vyse, marked on the airspeed indicator. If you exercise some discretion and limit the load to less than gross, these performance airspeeds can be improved upon. Plan on a reduction in airspeed of about one-half the percentage reduction in weight. For example, the maximum takeoff weight of a Beech Duchess is 3,900 pounds and its blue line airspeed is 86 knots. If you load a Duchess to 3,500 pounds, a reduction of about 10 percent, the best single-engine rate-of-climb speed is reduced by 5 percent to 82 knots.

USING PERFORMANCE CHARTS

Takeoff Distances

From your very first takeoff in a multiengine airplane, you should calculate the takeoff distance, the accelerate-stop and accelerate-go distances, and the single-engine climb rate. If the airplane is too heavy, the runway too short, or the obstacles too high, you should reconsider your decision to take off.

The takeoff distance chart, figure 4-16, is another chase-around graph that takes into account pressure altitude, temperature, weight, wind component, and obstacle height (if any). The conditions in the sample problem are instructive: a fairly high density altitude, temperature warmer than standard, and an airplane loaded to gross takeoff weight.

Note that for normal takeoffs the brakes are held while the power is brought up to maximum. Under the stated conditions, you would lean the mixture for best power after bringing the throttles up to takeoff power. Liftoff speed is given as 71 knots, which is Vsse, and the initial climb speed through 50 feet is 80 knots—slower than Vxse, which is given as 85 knots in the tabulation of emergency speeds for the Duchess. Moral: memorize the V-speeds in the front of the manual for the checkride, but fly the airplane at the speeds given in the performance section. It would appear that a runway at least 4,000 feet long would be about right for this takeoff, but we're not through yet.

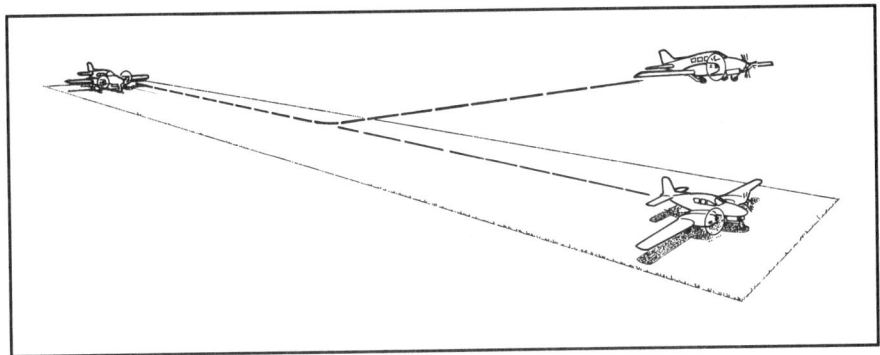

Figure 4-15. Accelerate-stop vs accelerate-go

Accelerate-Stop Distance

Accelerate-stop is a performance figure that allows you to determine whether the available runway is long enough for you to accelerate to decision speed, reject the takeoff, and bring the airplane to a stop without exploring the countryside. It is based on weight, pressure altitude, temperature, and wind. In many cases, the speed at which the engine is assumed to have failed varies with weight. This is not the case with all twins. For example, the Beech Duchess uses a speed of 71 knots at all weights. Figure 4-17, below, is a typical accelerate-stop chart, and it just happens to duplicate the normal takeoff chart sample conditions. According to the chart, you could begin your takeoff roll from the very end of a 4,000-foot-long runway, accelerate to 71 knots, lose an engine, and bring the airplane to a halt 750 feet from the departure end of the pavement—if you did everything right. My guess is that unless you enjoy the same perfect conditions as the factory test pilot did when the manual's figures were determined, you would need some assistance to get the airplane out of the dirt and back on the pavement. But could you have continued that takeoff? That calculation comes next.

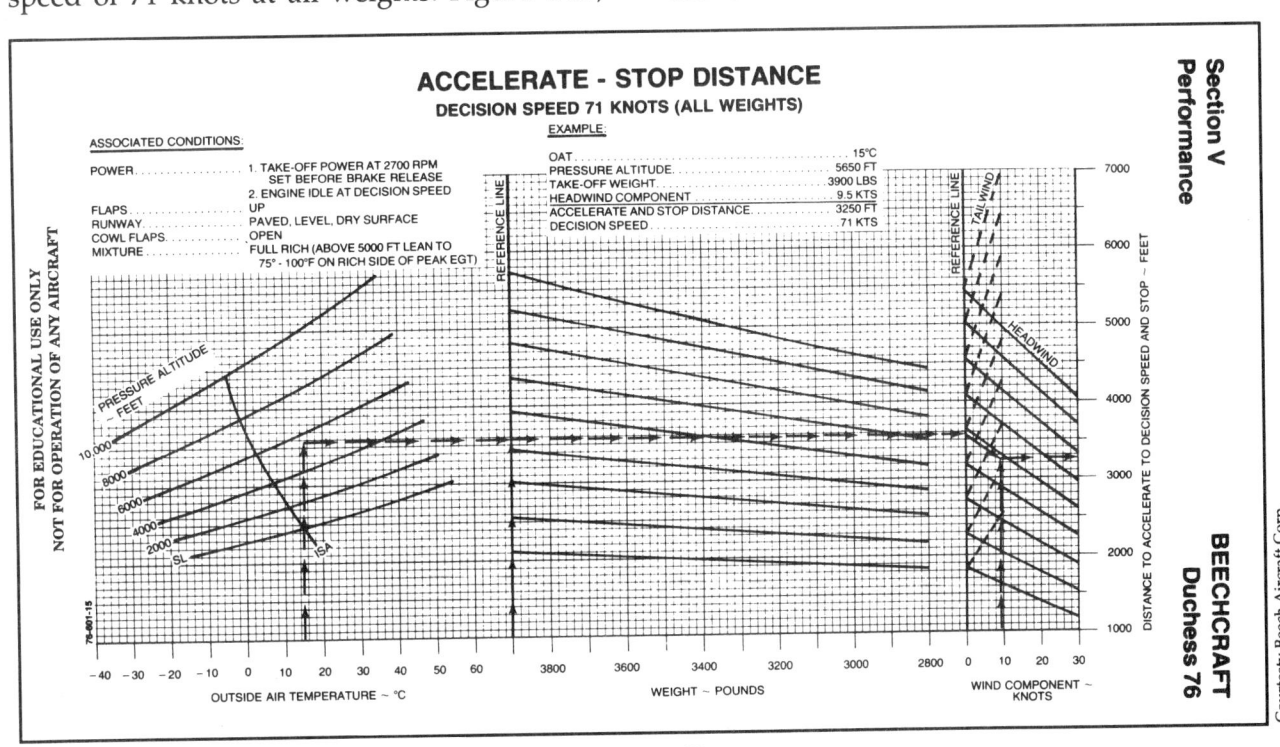

Figure 4-17.

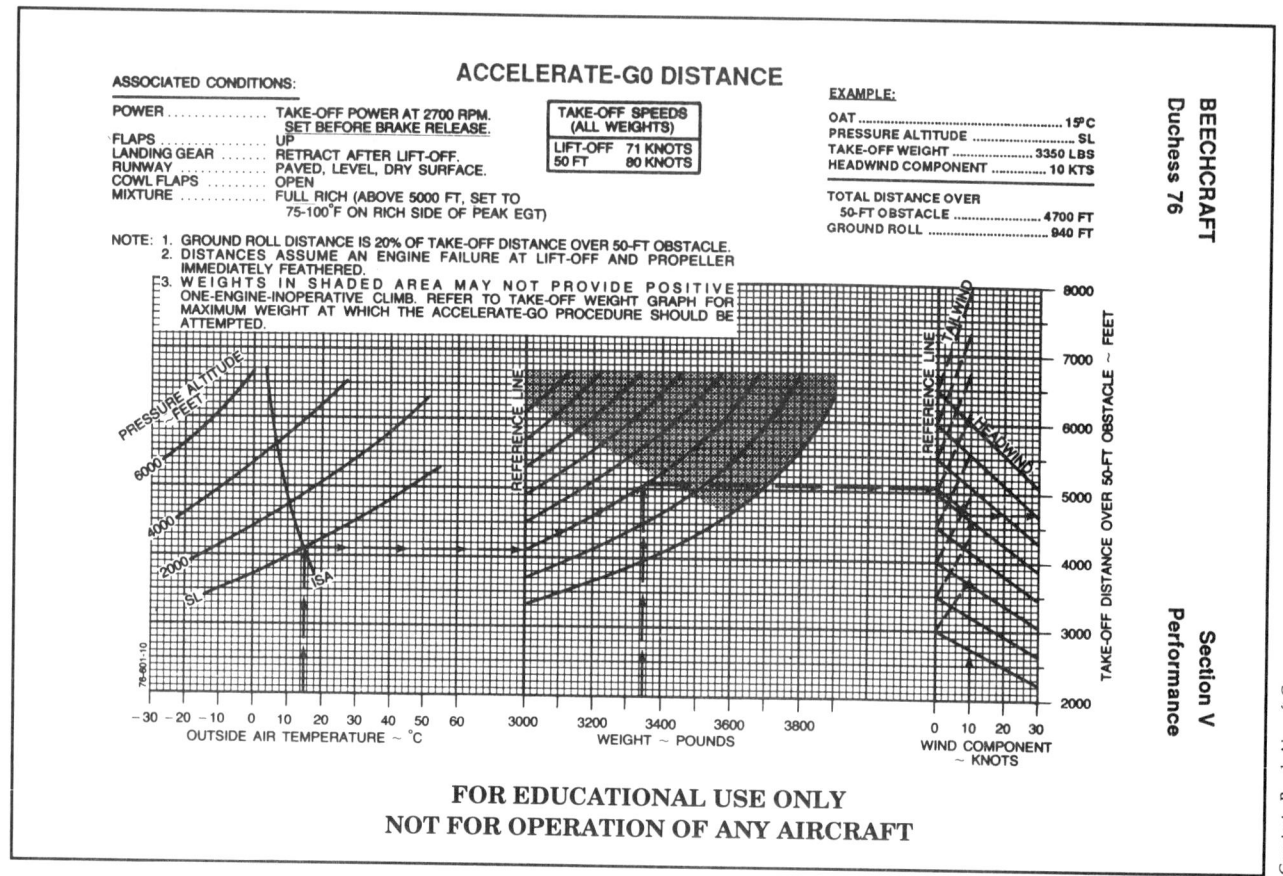

Figure 4-18.

Accelerate-Go

Accelerate-go is a performance figure based on a multiengine pilot's ability to accelerate to takeoff decision speed, lose an engine, continue the takeoff, and climb to clear a 50-foot obstacle. Figure 4-18 is used to determine it. As was the case with accelerate-stop, you need to know your aircraft's takeoff weight, the pressure altitude, temperature, and the wind component. Since Beechcraft didn't use the normal takeoff distance conditions for this graph, you will have to do it yourself.

Weight	3,900 lbs
PA	5,650 feet
Temperature	15 degrees Centigrade

9.5 knot headwind component

You don't have to get very far into the problem to learn that it isn't going to work. The intersection of 15 degrees and a 5,650-foot pressure altitude is up near the top of the graph, and a horizontal line over to the reference line runs right into the shaded area. This decision is a no-brainer: if you lose an engine at liftoff speed, you will have to get on the binders and screech to a stop. Any attempt to fly on one engine under these conditions will result in an off-airport landing at a spot not of your choosing.

Climb — One Engine Inoperative

Not willing to give up that easily? Go back and try the same conditions on figure 4-9. It doesn't take a very sharp pencil to see that the climb rate would be less than 50 feet per minute, a rate that would be eroded by any turbulence or maneuvering. Of course, you could have avoided all of this calculation by using the takeoff weight chart 4-1, which indicates that you would have to offload 1,000 pounds of fuel and/or passengers to have a fighting chance. Unfortunately, a take-

PLANNING AND PERFORMANCE

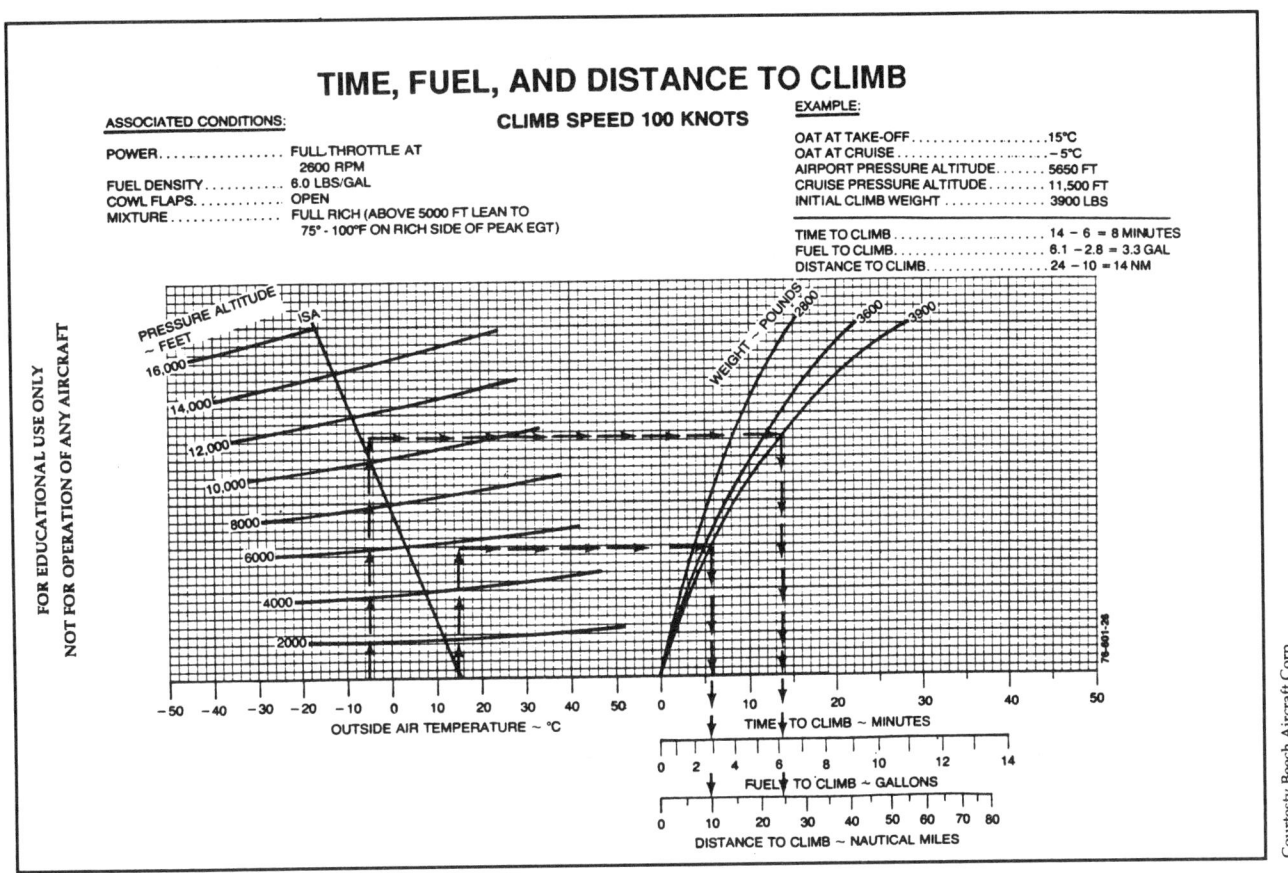

Figure 4-19.

off weight chart is not provided in all operating handbooks.

Note the steepness of the curves in the weight portion of the accelerate-go chart. Assuming a no-wind, standard day at sea level, a 10 percent increase in weight (from 3,300 pounds to 3,630 pounds) increases the accelerate-go distance by over 30 percent (from 4,900 feet to 6,500 feet). Consider that when your passengers show up with unexpected friends or extra baggage.

The manuals for some light twins do not include accelerate-go charts, which should serve as a warning that their manufacturers do not consider those airplanes capable of climbing after losing an engine.

Time, Fuel and Distance to Climb

Assuming that your takeoff distance calculations look good, the next planning step is to figure out how much fuel will be required to fly the trip and have legal reserves. Figure 4-19 looks complicated, but it isn't.

You can see that in the sample problem the departure airport still has a pressure altitude of 5,650 feet, the temperature is 15 degrees Centigrade, and the airplane still weighs 3,900 pounds. The lesson that was learned from the accelerate-go chart has not been ignored, necessarily, but the odds are in favor of going.

As you can see from the sample problem, the first step is to draw a vertical line from the outside air temperature at cruise altitude to the cruise altitude line, from that point horizontally to the weight, and then down to the baseline to read the time, fuel, and distance required if the departure airport was at sea level. The answers are 14 minutes, 6.1 gallons, and 24 miles.

The next step is to start at the baseline with the

4-15

surface temperature and draw a vertical line to the field elevation of the departure airport, then horizontally to the weight and down again to read time, fuel, and distance as if you hadn't climbed at all. That works out to be 6 minutes, 2.8 gallons, and 10 miles. Now subtract the second set of figures from the first set, and you have the time, fuel, and distance for a takeoff and climb from 5,650 feet to 11,500 feet: 8 minutes, 3.3 gallons, and 14 nautical miles. Your manual may also include an allowance for taxi fuel, which must be included in the total fuel burn.

These are important calculations, because your fuel burn calculations for the cruise segment will be in error if you don't account for the fact that you will have consumed some time, fuel, and distance by the time you reach cruise altitude. If the time to climb is more than 10 minutes for every hour at cruise altitude, rethink your choice of cruising altitude; fuel efficiency at that altitude will not overcome the increased fuel burned during the climb.

If you maintain a "howgozit" record (figure 4-20) of fuel consumption, as you complete your cruise checklist after leveling off, you will record the fact that the fuel on board has diminished by the quantity that you calculate using

Departure time	Time enroute	gph	gals burned	gals remaining
0830				100
Top of climb	:24	26	10.5	89
Cruise	2:30	16	40	50
Descent	:18	12	4	55

Figure 4-20. A "Howgozit" chart.

the Time, Fuel and Distance chart (be conservative) when you level off at cruise altitude.

Range and Endurance Profiles

These charts, figures 4-21 and 4-22, enable you to predict either how far your airplane will fly or how long it will stay up in the air on full tanks. The range chart is based on zero wind at altitude and, accordingly, its predictions should be taken as advisory only. The endurance chart is more objective in nature; if it predicts an endurance of 6 hours at a given altitude and power setting, you had better have a descent clearance in hand well before 6 hours have elapsed.

It is very unlikely that the winds at cruise altitude will be calm, and you should consider the forecast wind in the planning process. To be conservative, use 150 percent of a forecast headwind or only 50 percent of a forecast tailwind. If the wind is forecast to be quartering, rather than directly ahead or behind, use half of the value you got from applying the headwind/tailwind rule.

Using the charts is simple: draw a horizontal line from your cruise pressure altitude to the line representing the cruise power setting and drop a vertical line to the base of the graph to read either range or endur-

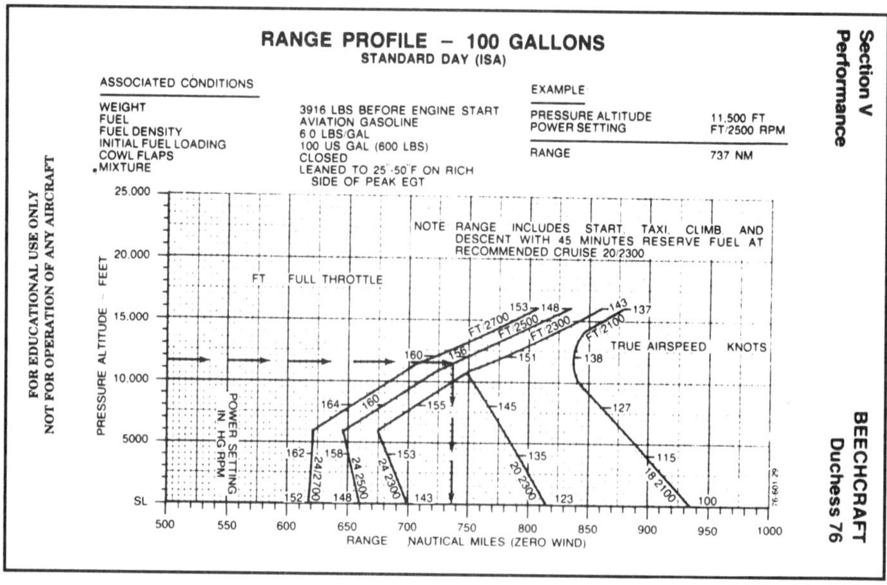

Figure 4-21.

PLANNING AND PERFORMANCE

ance. Each is predicated on the temperature at each pressure altitude level being the standard temperature for that level.

The charts themselves are instructive, however. Note how the lines for the higher power settings bend at about 6,000 feet — that is where you will have the throttles full forward. The lines that slope upward from that altitude are all full throttle power settings. Each line has true airspeed (TAS) markings to enable you to predict the TAS at that altitude and power setting. Can you see why 20 inches and 2,300 RPM is a favorite cruise setting for many Duchess pilots? The flight might take a little longer at 20/2,300, but the increase in range and endurance at pressure altitudes below 10,000 feet is well worth it.

Cruise Power Tables

These tables allow you to fine-tune your planning for non-standard conditions. Look back at

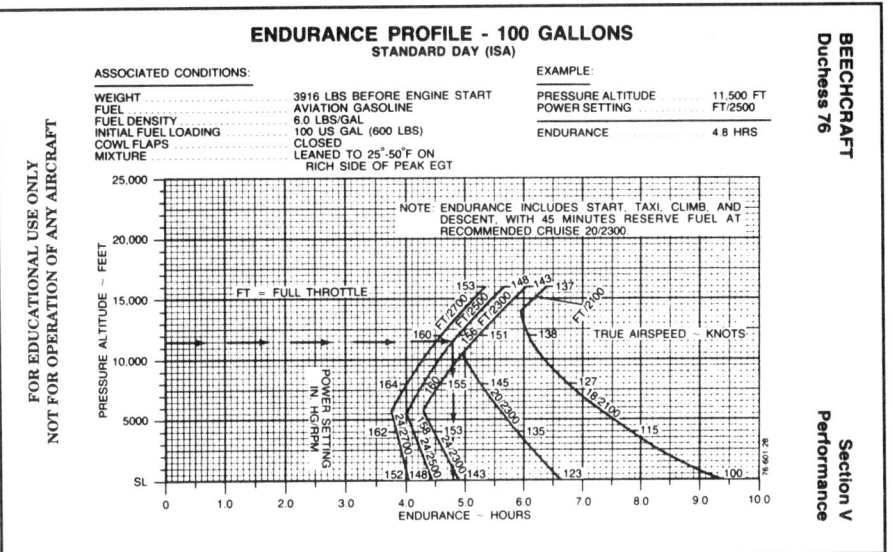

Figure 4-22.

the accelerate-stop, accelerate-go, or takeoff distance charts, and you will see a line marked "ISA" (International Standard Atmosphere) crossing through the pressure altitude lines. That line represents the standard temperature for each altitude, starting with 15 degrees Centigrade at sea level. The Flight Service Station briefer will give you the forecast temperature at your selected cruising altitude, and you can determine whether it is warmer or colder than the standard temperature.

RECOMMENDED CRUISE POWER - 24.0 IN. HG @ 2300 RPM (OR FULL THROTTLE)

PRESS ALT FEET	ISA −20°C (−36°F)						STANDARD DAY (ISA)						ISA +20°C (+36°F)					
	IOAT °C	IOAT °F	MAN. PRESS IN.HG	FUEL FLOW/ENGINE PPH	FUEL FLOW/ENGINE GPH	IAS KTS	TAS KTS	IOAT °C	IOAT °F	MAN. PRESS IN.HG	FUEL FLOW/ENGINE PPH	FUEL FLOW/ENGINE GPH	IAS KTS	TAS KTS	IOAT °C	IOAT °F	MAN. PRESS IN.HG	FUEL FLOW/ENGINE PPH	FUEL FLOW/ENGINE GPH	IAS KTS	TAS KTS

PRESS ALT FEET	IOAT °C	IOAT °F	MAN. PRESS IN.HG	PPH	GPH	IAS KTS	TAS KTS	IOAT °C	IOAT °F	MAN. PRESS IN.HG	PPH	GPH	IAS KTS	TAS KTS	IOAT °C	IOAT °F	MAN. PRESS IN.HG	PPH	GPH	IAS KTS	TAS KTS
SL	-3	27	24.0	55	9.2	147	142	17	63	24.0	53	8.8	143	143	37	99	24.0	51	8.5	139	144
1000	-5	23	24.0	56	9.3	147	144	15	59	24.0	54	9.0	143	145	35	95	24.0	52	8.7	139	146
2000	-7	19	24.0	57	9.5	148	147	13	55	24.0	55	9.2	143	148	33	91	24.0	53	8.8	139	149
3000	-9	16	24.0	58	9.7	148	149	11	52	24.0	56	9.3	144	150	31	88	24.0	54	9.0	139	151
4000	-11	12	24.0	59	9.8	148	152	9	48	24.0	57	9.5	144	153	29	84	24.0	55	9.2	140	153
5000	-13	9	24.0	60	10.0	148	154	7	45	24.0	58	9.7	144	155	27	81	24.0	56	9.3	140	156
6000	-15	5	23.7	61	10.2	148	156	5	41	23.7	59	9.8	144	157	25	77	23.7	57	9.5	140	158
7000	-17	1	22.8	59	9.8	145	155	3	37	22.8	57	9.5	141	156	23	73	22.8	55	9.2	137	157
8000	-19	-2	21.9	57	9.5	142	154	1	34	21.9	55	9.2	138	155	21	70	21.9	53	8.8	134	156
9000	-21	-6	21.1	55	9.2	139	153	-1	30	21.1	53	8.8	135	154	19	66	21.1	51	8.5	131	155
10,000	-23	-9	20.3	53	8.8	136	152	-3	27	20.3	51	8.5	132	153	17	63	20.3	49	8.2	127	154
11,000	-25	-13	19.5	51	8.5	133	151	-5	23	19.5	49	8.2	129	152	15	59	19.5	47	7.8	124	152
12,000	-27	-17	18.8	49	8.2	130	150	-7	19	18.8	47	7.8	125	151	13	55	18.8	46	7.7	121	151
13,000	-29	-20	18.0	47	7.8	127	148	-9	16	18.0	46	7.7	122	149	11	52	18.0	44	7.3	117	149
14,000	-31	-24	17.3	45	7.5	123	147	-11	12	17.3	44	7.3	119	147	9	48	17.3	42	7.0	114	147
15,000	-33	-27	16.7	44	7.3	120	145	-13	9	16.7	42	7.0	115	145	7	45	16.7	41	6.8	110	144
16,000	-35	-31	16.0	42	7.0	116	143	-15	5	16.0	40	6.7	111	143	5	41	16.0	39	6.5	106	142

NOTES:
1. Full throttle manifold pressure settings are approximate.
2. Shaded area represents operation with full throttle.
3. Lean to 25° - 50°F on rich side of peak EGT.
4. Cruise speeds are presented at an average weight of 3600 lbs.

Figure 4-23.

4-17

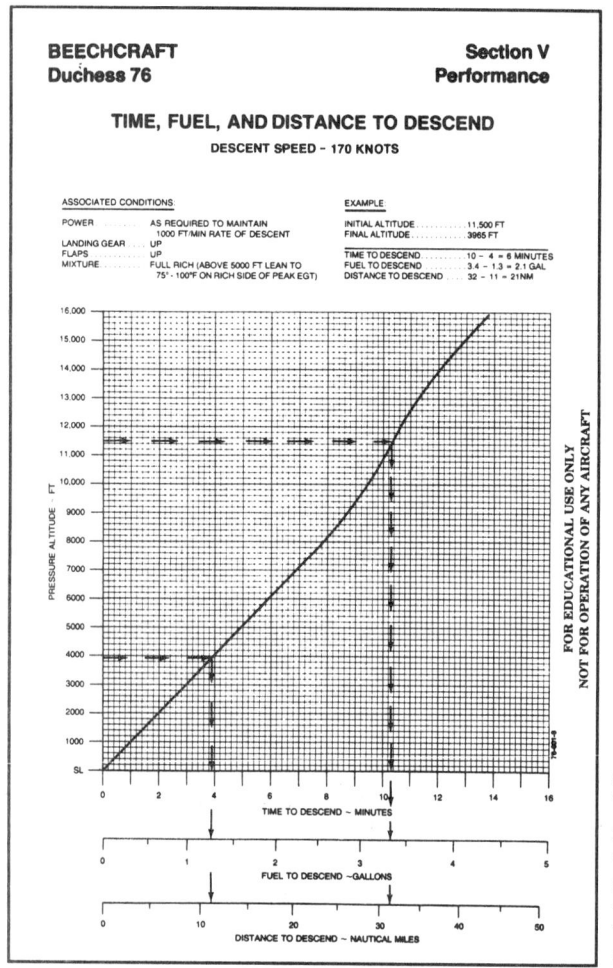

Figure 4-24.

Figure 4-23, on the previous page, says that at 10,000 feet on a standard day (outside air temperature -5 degrees Centigrade), full throttle and 2,400 RPM will give you an indicated airspeed (IAS) of 132 knots (TAS 153 knots) while burning 8.5 gallons-per-hour per engine. The briefer, however, told you that the forecast temperature for that altitude was 2 degrees Centigrade, 7 degrees warmer than standard. Now what can you expect for speed and fuel burn?

The columns on the right side of the chart are for a temperature 20 degrees warmer than standard, and the indicated airspeed at that temperature is 127 knots, a difference of 5 knots. For every degree of temperature increase above standard, the IAS decreases 5/20 or .25 knot. If the forecast temperature is 7 degrees warmer than standard, the IAS will decrease by 7 x .25 or 1.75 knots. Too much trouble? Just eyeball it, then. The temperature increase is about half of 20 degrees, so figure that the airspeed will fall halfway between 132 and 127 and that the fuel burn will fall halfway between 8.5 and 8.2 gallons-per-hour per engine. Use the degree of accuracy you feel comfortable with, but always be conservative. Round the fuel burn up to the next highest whole gallon-per-hour and you'll have some fuel in the bank.

Descent Planning

The manufacturer provides a chart of time, fuel, and distance to descend (figure 4-24). It is similar to the Time, Fuel, and Distance chart for the climb to altitude in that you look up two sets of numbers and subtract one from the other to get the information for your flight. First, draw a horizontal line from your cruise altitude to the reference line and from that point, drop vertically to the baseline to read the time, fuel, and distance for a descent from cruise altitude all the way to sea level.

Repeat the process, using the field elevation of the destination airport, to determine how much time, fuel, and distance would be required to descend from field elevation to sea level, and subtract those figures from the first set to get the information you want. You now know that the distance you will fly at cruise altitude is the point-to-point measurement from your navigational chart minus the calculated distances for climb and descent, so you can figure the total time enroute using that distance at cruise speed plus the times you got from the climb and descent charts. You also have a handle on the total fuel required and can enter your fuel order. And you have two conflicting desires: to have more than enough fuel on board and to try to stay well below max. gross weight. Good luck.

CHAPTER FIVE

TAKEOFF AND DEPARTURE

YOUR PLANNING IS COMPLETE, THE AIRPLANE IS loaded, and it's time to taxi out for takeoff. The takeoff phase of flight is generally perceived to be the most hazardous, no matter how many engines your airplane has. It's time for constructive paranoia.

Paranoia is defined in part as a tendency toward excessive suspiciousness or distrustfulness, and if your Aviation Medical Examiner thinks that you are paranoid, you won't be issued a medical certificate. No matter. When you are the pilot of a multiengine airplane, a little paranoia can save your bacon.

Most pilots will go through an entire flying career without having an engine failure, but that is no reason for complacency. The Golden Rule of multiengine flying is this: convince yourself that you will have an engine failure at some point during every takeoff and be ready for it. You won't know which engine will fail or at what point in the takeoff the failure will occur, but always expect a failure.

This is my reasoning: Medical experts who try to figure out why pilots do the things they do have identified four stages in an engine-out emergency. The first, confusion, lasts about 3 seconds; during this period the pilot experiences either an unexpected reaction to a control input or gets no reaction at all. This, quite understandably, is confusing.

It takes 2 more seconds for the pilot to realize that the cause of the problem is that an engine has failed. This is the recognition phase. For 1 more second the pilot's reaction is, "No, this can't be happening to me!" This is called the denial phase. After 7 seconds have elapsed, the

pilot begins to take the appropriate action, if the airplane has not already hit the ground or become uncontrollable.

The most effective way to avoid having these four stages end in disaster is to expect a failure on every takeoff. For example, there will be no confusion phase if you convince yourself that every unusual noise, vibration, or steering difficulty is caused by engine failure and make mental preparations to react appropriately. Just what you should do depends on where you are in the takeoff and climb procedure, and we will discuss that in detail. Recognition becomes acceptance: you knew it was going to happen, and it did. No lost time. The same is true of denial. You can't deny that something is happening when you expected it all the time. That brings you to the action phase without losing 7 seconds.

During the takeoff roll, and when airborne with the gear down and runway available, the appropriate action is to stop the airplane straight ahead. If that means running off the departure end of the runway and banging up the airplane, so be it. It is better to hit something while at 30 knots and decelerating than to fall 100 feet out of control.

You are most vulnerable when the airspeed needle is between the red line (Vmc) and the blue line (Vyse), and once airborne, you should accelerate through that area as quickly as possible. Once the gear is retracted or in transit (this should not happen until there is no longer any usable runway), you should consider yourself committed to continue. Some airplanes (the Seneca series is an example) are ready to fly before the airspeed needle reaches the red line, and if you apply forward pressure to stay on the ground until Vsse, you will end up wheelbarrowing along with the nose strut compressed and little or no weight on the mains. In those airplanes, you have to let the airplane fly when it is ready, and accept the fact that you are momentarily vulnerable.

There is no set procedure if you lose an engine while in the area of vulnerability between the red and blue lines. That is why pretakeoff planning is important. Do you put it back down in an area that you know is available beneath the takeoff path? Do you climb straight ahead for ten miles while struggling up to pattern altitude? There are no pat answers, because every situation will be different. You must have a plan and stick to that plan.

If you will be taking off into instrument meteorological conditions, consider the climb rate required for the departure procedure. Could you make it on one engine? Is the weather at the departure airport good enough for you to make a "no sweat" single-engine approach? Where is the nearest airport with VFR conditions? Can you handle an engine-out emergency under IFR? Be hard on yourself.

Calculating Climb Rates Before Takeoff

Will obstruction clearance be a problem for this takeoff? Every manufacturer lists airspeeds for

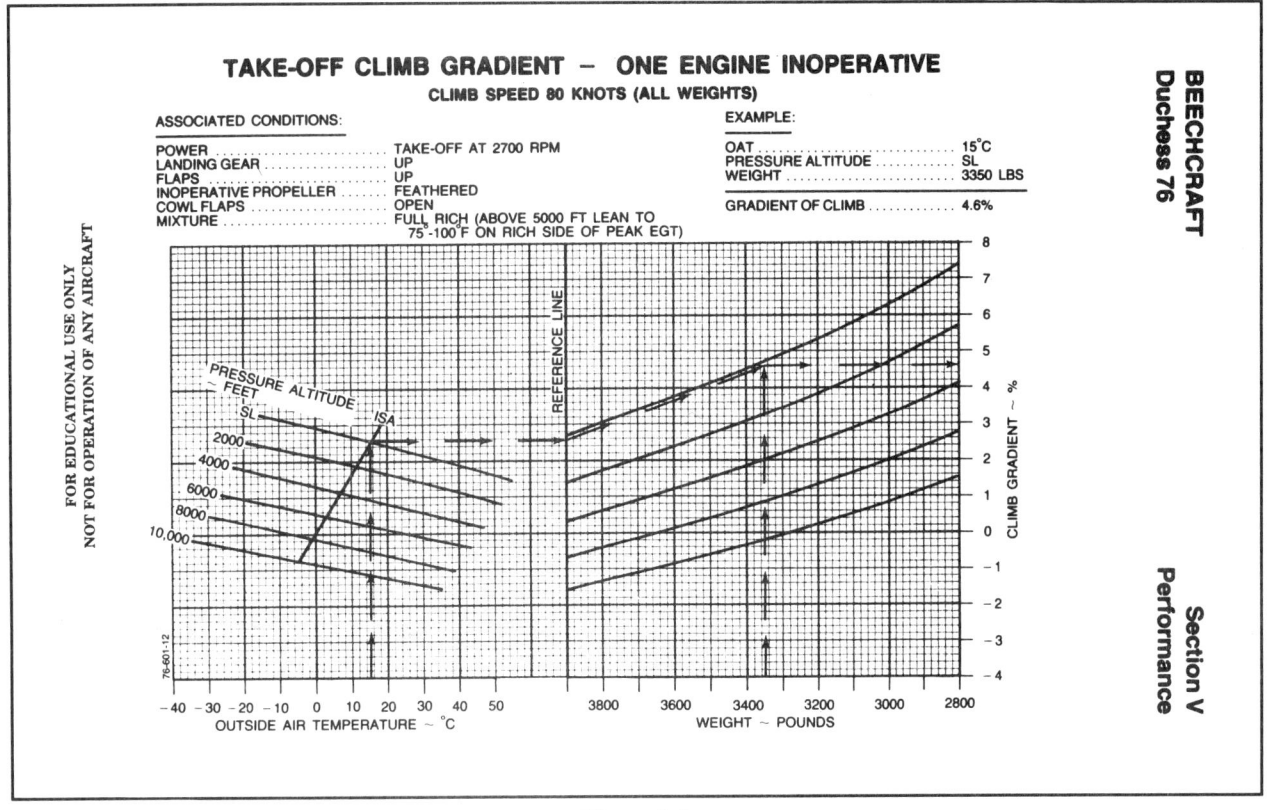

Figure 5-1.

best all-engine angle-of-climb and for best single-engine rate-of-climb, using the FAA standard 50 foot obstacle as the hurdle you are going to try to jump. Figure 5-1 allows you to calculate just how many feet of altitude you will gain per 1000 feet of horizontal distance *if* you follow the procedure recommended by the POH. This is the climb gradient, or slope, not the rate-of-climb.

As you can see from the sample problem, a Duchess taking off from a sea level airport on a standard day at a gross weight of 3,350 pounds (550 pounds below maximum gross weight) can lose an engine at rotation, have its pilot clean up the airplane, climb at 80 knots (which is slower than Vxse), and gain 46 feet of altitude per 1000 feet of forward progress in no-wind conditions. That's about 276 feet per mile, or 368 feet per minute, during the initial climb. Not much, especially when you consider that it is based on everything being done perfectly.

Unless the runway you are departing from is really short, with that 50-foot tree or apartment house right at the departure end (which brings your judgment into question), the smartest action you could take following a failure immediately after liftoff is to put the airplane back down again, accepting the possibility of damage and injuries. Too many pilots expose themselves and their passengers to the possibility of a fatal accident in attempts to get the airplane back on the ground without a scratch. If you have done your accelerate-stop and accelerate-go calculations, (see Chapter 4) you will have a good idea of what you can accomplish safely. The climb-gradient chart gives you an idea of how much clearance you will have over those apartment houses 2 miles from the end of the runway.

Figure 5-2, on the following page, assumes that you have cleared all of the close-in obstacles and want to climb to a safe altitude with the gear and flaps up and the dead engine's propeller feathered. Note that the airspeed is now 85 knots, the single-engine best rate-of-climb speed. Using the same conditions that were used to determine the engine-out climb gradient (3,350

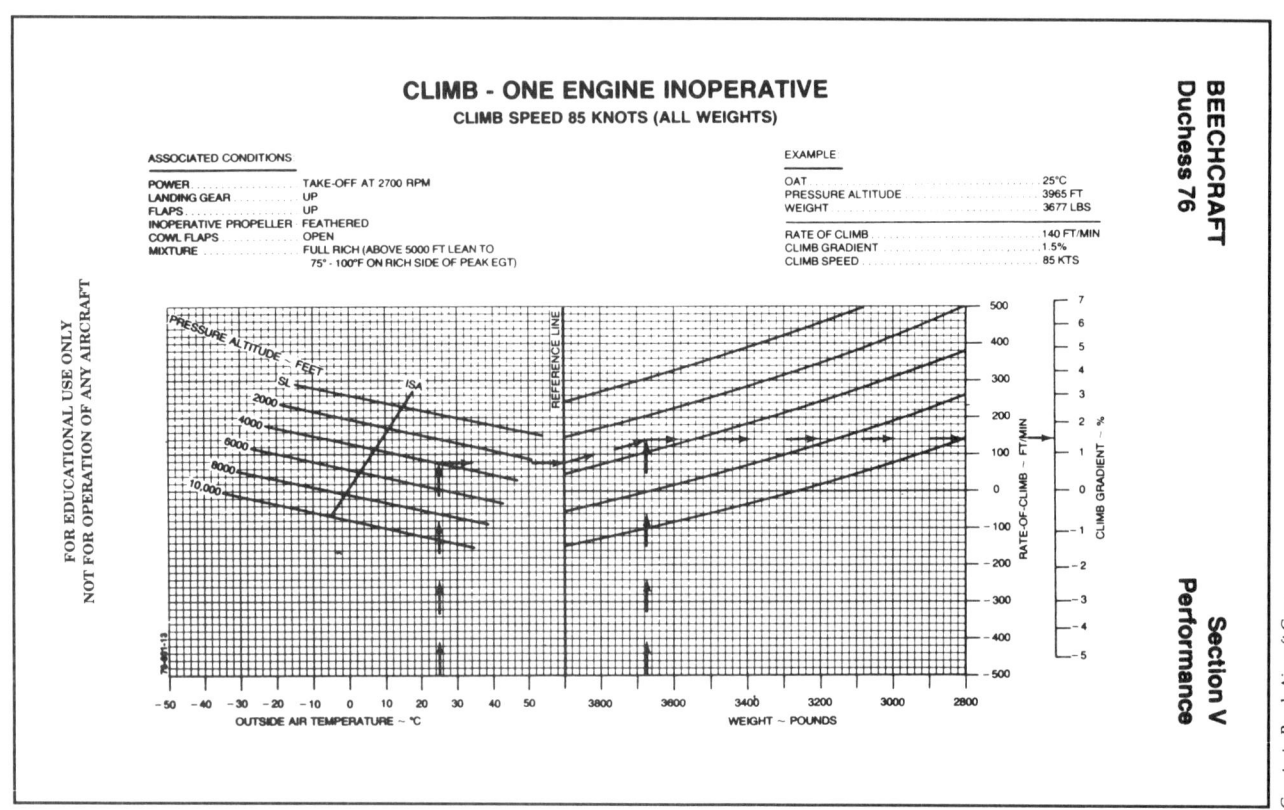

Figure 5-2.

pounds on a standard day at sea level), the rate of climb improves to about 420 feet-per-minute. Considering that any turning will erode this minimal climb performance, how far from the airport will you be when you have gained enough altitude to maneuver?

The Takeoff Roll

Do not accept an intersection takeoff, and when you are cleared for takeoff from the hold line, don't sacrifice runway distance by making a rolling takeoff. Use every foot of the available runway by taxiing toward the end of the paved surface and then turning to align the airplane with the runway. As the airplane accelerates, check the fuel flow and exhaust gas temperature gauges — they will be better indicators of impending problems than any other instruments. The power instruments may mislead you, for the following reasons. During the takeoff roll, manifold pressure will be at or near ambient outside pressure (non-turbocharged airplanes, of course), and prop speed will be near the red line. When an engine fails, its manifold pressure gauge will read ambient outside pressure, which will be very close to the full-throttle manifold pressure — looking at the MAP gauge will not tell you which engine has failed. Similarly, unless the engine has experienced massive internal damage, the propeller will not spin down immediately, so looking to the tachometer for clues is not a good idea.

As the airplane nears rotation speed, the pressure differential between the inside and outside of the fuselage will reach the point at which poorly latched access or baggage compartment doors will open, or at which the end of a seat belt hanging outside a door will set up an ear-splitting racket. Be ready to pull the throttles back to the stops in either case. Maybe you will hear an unintelligible transmission on the radio; was it "Have a nice flight!" or was it "Your left engine has black smoke coming out of it!"? If you don't know, stop the airplane and find out what was said.

When the airspeed needle reaches Vmc plus 5

knots (for most twins), rotate to a positive climb attitude — and be ready for an engine to fail before the airspeed reaches the blue line. With the VSI needle indicating a climb rate of at least 300 feet-per-minute, lower the nose slightly and accelerate to Vy, the best all-engine rate-of-climb speed. The rationale for using Vy is that there will be an unavoidable loss of airspeed as you react to a failure, and a deceleration from Vy to Vyse won't cause the problems that slowing from Vyse toward Vmc might cause.

Engine Fails!

But imagine that despite your best plans and lucky rabbit's foot, the left engine burps twice and quits just as the altimeter indicates that you are 100 feet above the ground. The airplane swerves hard to the left and begins to roll in that direction. Reacting instinctively, you rotate the yoke all the way to the right — and lose directional control. Why?

The purpose of flight training is to substitute trained reactions for instinctive reactions, isn't it? Let's go back to the instant of failure and start over, using trained reactions. As the airplane swerves and rolls to the left, you push the right rudder pedal all the way to the floorboard, stopping the turn. Simultaneously, you apply enough right aileron to establish a bank into the good engine and regain directional control by developing a horizontal lift component to offset the turning moment. This time, you don't lose control.

Tests by the FAA have shown that it takes a bank of at least 5 degrees toward the good engine to overcome the initial roll and maintain control of the airplane (the "not more than 5 degrees" you may have heard is a certification limitation placed on the manufacturer when the published minimum control speed is determined). This establishes a slight sideslip into the good engine, and because the airplane is slipping toward the fully deflected rudder, the increased airflow makes the rudder more effective. You can bank more than 5 degrees, and make the rudder so effective that you can almost give your foot a rest.

Figure 5-3. Lots of rudder and just enough aileron

Unfortunately, this good medicine has bad side effects. Increasing the bank eats into climb performance at a time when you have none to spare, with a 10 degree bank completely eliminating any climb capability. With the airplane under control, however, climb performance will be improved if you relax the aileron pressure and reduce the bank to about 3 degrees (or less, depending on a lot of variables. Just don't level the wings completely).

Because the conditions that create zero sideslip can vary from one airplane to another, you can determine the best combination of bank angle and ball deflection by taping a piece of string to the nose of the airplane (glider pilots call it a yaw string). Zero sideslip has been attained when the loose end of the string streams straight back, parallel to the longitudinal axis. Without a yaw string, the slip/skid indicator is a better guide to being "just right" than is the attitude indicator at these small bank angles; the ball should be about halfway out of its cage on the good engine side, and the turn coordinator should be showing zero rate of turn.

The best performance indicator is the vertical speed indicator, because the goal of all of this drag reduction is to enable the crippled airplane to climb out of danger. Don't forget that the horizontal component of lift isn't a gift — it comes from a reduction in vertical lift (figure 5-3 on previous page).

While your right foot has been exerting 150 pounds of pressure on its rudder pedal and your left hand has been busy rolling the airplane into the good engine — remember, it was the left engine that failed — your right hand has not been idle. Its duty, whenever you suspect an engine failure, is to move across the throttle quadrant from right to left (Pilots of older Beech aircraft please bear with me for a while), pushing the mixture and prop controls full forward and adding sufficient power to avoid loss of altitude. Figure 5-4 shows the sequence.

Many instructors (and the FAA's Flight Training Handbook) advocate pushing both throttles full forward in every situation. I suggest a more reasoned approach — as reasoned as you can get when you are in a crisis situation. Full power is great when you are in a takeoff or climb situation close to the ground. It is not necessary if an engine fails in cruising flight, and full power on one side will drive the airplane off of the localizer and glideslope if used during an ILS approach. Add just enough power to avoid losing altitude or slowing below Vyse and yet enough to develop sufficient differential rudder pressure for you to identify the failed engine. I like author Richard L. Taylor's advice: go to the next higher power setting. If you have set climb power, go to takeoff power; if you have set cruise power, go to climb power; if you are on an approach, go to cruise power.

Cleaning Up the Airplane

You have done all you can on the thrust side of the equation, so drag reduction comes next. Form the habit of always checking the gear and flap position. You are most vulnerable during takeoff and initial climb, when the gear is extended and the flaps, if they are used at all, are

Figure 5-4. Right-to-left at the instant of failure

in the takeoff position. The gear-flap sequence varies between different airplane models, but more often than not, the manufacturer calls for gear retraction first, since the flap setting for takeoff creates more lift than drag. If the gear retraction sequence involves doors that must open to accept the wheels, as is the case with the Cessna Skymaster, the drag caused by the sudden appearance of cavernous holes in the bottom of the fuselage is the reason that the landing gear is not retracted immediately.

The sequence for securing a failed engine is IDENTIFY, VERIFY, FEATHER. You IDENTIFY the dead engine by rudder pressure; one foot is pressing the rudder pedal on the good engine side nearly to the firewall (and your leg muscles are beginning to ache), while the other foot is idle. The memory aid is: dead foot = dead engine. In our example, the left engine has given up the ghost and your left foot is doing absolutely nothing. You VERIFY by retarding the throttle of the engine that you have identified while listening for a change in engine sound and checking for a change in rudder pressure. If you can pull the throttle back without any apparent change, you have verified that the left engine has failed. The last step is to FEATHER the propeller on the engine that you have IDEN-

Figure 5-5. Left-to-right to secure the failed engine

Figure 5-6. Baron power levers

TIFIED and VERIFIED. Figure 5-5 shows the sequence for securing the dead engine. With those items taken care of and the airplane under control, everything else is housekeeping. You will want to pull the failed engine's mixture control to idle cutoff. If the airplane is equipped with cowl flaps, open them on the good engine side. Get out the manufacturer's checklist and follow its recommendations for securing the electrical system. The emergency is over. All you have to do now is get the airplane to a suitable location for landing.

The control sequence for securing the failed engine in the last paragraph (throttle, propeller, mixture) agrees with the recommended procedure in almost all piston twins. You may find an owner's manual or text that counsels that the sequence should be throttle, mixture, propeller. Your instructor and examiner might say that you should follow the manual in every case, or they might opt for standardization. Piper says that either method is acceptable. Cessna, for reasons that I assume have to do with product liability, makes no such concession. All Beechcraft twins use the throttle, prop, mixture sequence. In my opinion, standardization of procedures reduces the possibility of error as you transition from one type of twin to another.

There is at least one good reason to delay pulling the mixture until the propeller has been feathered: pilots aren't perfect. If you inadvertently retard the wrong throttle or propeller control, the change in engine noise will alert you to the error and you can correct it quickly. However, if you inadvertently lean the mixture on the operating engine to idle cutoff, and, upon hearing it begin to spin down, push the mixture back to full rich, the odds are that you are going to hear a dandy backfire. Why blow the exhaust system off a perfectly good engine? You have enough trouble already. If you save the mixture for the securing phase, after aircraft control has been regained, you can take the time to look for the correct mixture control. The Duchess manual, which we have been using as a reference throughout this book, lumps pulling the mixture to idle cutoff in with such housekeeping measures as closing the cowl flaps and turning off the magnetos and alternator.

Those of you who fly older Beechcraft twins deserve an explanation. The quadrant layout on older Beeches is, from left to right, propeller, throttle, mixture (figure 5-6). You can see why my left-to-right instructions wouldn't work. Newer Beechcraft twins, such as the Duchess, follow the now conventional quadrant layout.

The securing procedure described above did not mention taking any action with regard to the fuel selectors, because unless the engine is on fire, there is no immediate requirement to shut off the fuel. Crossfeeding the operating engine from tanks on the dead engine side is not usually required until lateral imbalance demands it or until that fuel is needed to get the airplane to a safe landing spot. It is really a cruise consideration, not something you must think of at takeoff time. Most, but not all, crossfeed procedures call for the fuel selector on the dead engine side to be placed in the OFF position, and the fuel selector on the operating engine side to be placed in CROSSFEED. There are enough differences between different airplanes, however (the Twin Comanche and Beech Travel Air come to mind), that you should check the crossfeed procedure for your airplane before you need it.

With the airplane airborne, gear and flaps up and the offending propeller feathered, you are either on your way back to the airport, or, if weather conditions will not permit you to return and land, you are enroute to your takeoff alternate. You did have a takeoff alternate in mind, didn't you?

CHAPTER SIX

CRUISING FLIGHT

The Cruise Checklist

CRUISING FLIGHT IS WHERE HAVING TWO OPERATing engines pays off, because the excess power that got you to altitude at a brisk rate of climb can now be converted into forward speed. Your job becomes one of monitoring systems so that the cruise portion of the flight will be accomplished with maximum efficiency.

If your airplane's Pilot's Operating Handbook does not have a cruise checklist, you should make up your own. Among the items on such a checklist would be switching to the auxiliary or tip tanks, closing the cowl flaps, and setting the power and mixture. Be sure to check the procedure for the fuel pump switches — some models suggest that the fuel pumps be left in the "low" position when cruising above 12,000 feet. Never turn both fuel pump switches off simultaneously. If an engine-driven pump has failed while the electric pumps were performing their backup function and you kill them both at once, there will be a moment of confusion when that pump's engine begins to wind down. Far better to turn one pump off, wait ten seconds or so, and then turn the other pump off. You would be surprised at how long it takes for an engine to consume the fuel in the plumbing.

Before you reach for the fuel selectors, however, be sure that you understand how to manage your airplane's fuel system. In many airplanes with fuel-injected engines, fuel vapor and excess fuel from the engines returns to the main tanks, and if you haven't been on the mains long enough to make room for the return fuel, it will be vented overboard. Not good for fuel planning. In these situations (the Cessna 310 comes to mind) the Pilot's Operating Handbook will require that you continue to burn fuel out of the main tanks for a specified period of time before switching to auxiliary or tip tanks.

Most operating handbooks are noncommittal about cowl flaps, simply telling you to use them as required to maintain cylinder head temperatures within limits. Don't make closing the cowl flaps an automatic action without checking the cylinder head temperatures. Unless air pressure on the open cowl flaps at cruise speed will cause vibration or possible damage, leave them open for a few moments after leveling off at cruise altitude. The engines have been working hard and deserve an extra shot of cooling air before you close the cowl flaps completely. You might even want to close them in increments to moderate the temperature change.

When it comes time to set cruise power, you have many options. Don't be put off by the myth about never having the manifold pressure in inches be a larger number than the RPM in hundreds. This hoary old story, based on experience with radial engines, has no place in modern aircraft. Figure 6-1 shows an acceptable operating area with manifold pressures greater than RPM by four: 28 inches and 2,400 RPM fall into this area. The manufacturer's recommended cruise power settings are more conservative, with 24 inches over 2,300 RPM the largest gap. The Duchess'es 180-horsepower Lycomings do not differ greatly from other normally aspirated engines in their cruise power settings.

During World War II, Colonel Charles Lindbergh passed on to military pilots some power management techniques he had refined from his history-making transatlantic flight, and the methods he taught allowed our fighter and bomber pilots to stretch the range of their aircraft. Simply put, the rule was low propeller speed and high manifold pressure. In the days of radial engines, 1,600-1,700 RPM was considered low. The manufacturers of today's flat opposed engines consider 2,100 RPM as being low for cruise power. The tradeoff you must consider is high manifold pressure and low RPM versus low manifold pressure and high RPM.

A pilot who assumes that using low manifold pressure and high RPM will extend engine life is 180 degrees out of phase. Without sufficient pressure in the cylinder, the pistons will rattle up and down and the rings will scrape and scar

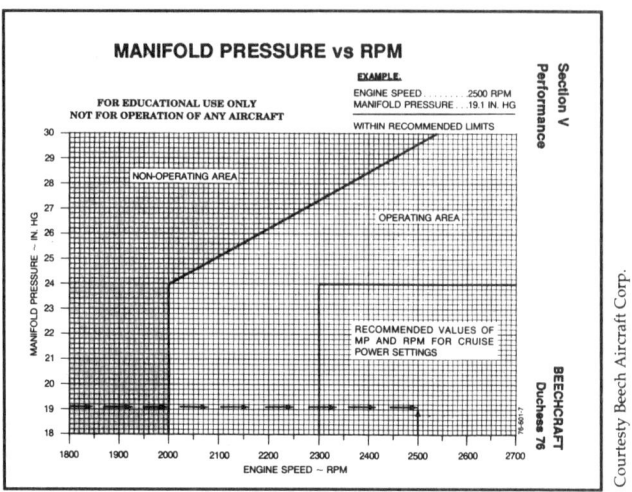

Figure 6-1.

the cylinder walls. That may be a slight exaggeration, but you get the picture. Piston ring flutter is a result of this type of operation, and nothing good will come from a piston ring that is not being allowed to do its job.

Take a few moments to analyze Figure 6-2 (cruise power chart). Note that for a given manifold pressure, reducing propeller speed cuts both true airspeed and fuel flow. However, the percentage reduction in fuel flow is twice the airspeed penalty. For example, if, while pulling 28 inches of manifold pressure, you reduce horsepower from 75 percent to 64 percent through use of a lower prop speed (2,500 down to 2,200), you will burn 15 percent less fuel while only losing 8 percent true airspeed.

The most efficient enroute altitude for normally aspirated airplanes is between 6,000 and 8,000 feet at 75 percent power. Within that range you will find the highest altitude at which 75 percent power can be maintained and also the highest true airspeed for a given rate of fuel consumption. I'm not recommending that you operate at 75 percent, however; if you use lower power settings, in addition to the reduction in fuel burn mentioned above, the optimum altitude will increase. You will find that 55 percent power gives the best tradeoff between speed and fuel economy.

Depending on the make and model of twin you are flying, you may not be able to determine the exact percentage horsepower that a given combination of manifold pressure and propeller speed will deliver. Some Operating Handbooks are silent on the subject, and you will have to refer to the engine manufacturer's manual for that information.

Throughout this book, I have suggested that you go by the numbers in the Pilot's Operating Handbook. When it comes to setting cruise power, however, there are several combinations of numbers to choose from. An excellent rule to follow is this: use the lowest prop speed at which the engines run smoothly, without noise or vibration. Based on my own experience, I suggest that you standardize on 2,300 RPM. With normally aspirated engines at cruise altitudes above 5,000 feet, you will be able to open the throttles fully without exceeding 75 percent power if you leave the props at 2,300 RPM.

There is another plus to operating at low RPM: if the pistons are traveling up and down at a leisurely pace, the fuel-air mixture will spend more time in the cylinder, cooling it down before the compression stroke begins.

Lean to the book fuel flow for the power setting you are using; if an EGT gauge or other source of analytical information is available, of course, use that information to the fullest extent. You will seldom go wrong by leaning to 50 degrees on the rich side of peak exhaust gas temperature, and Lycoming says that you can operate their engines at peak if the cylinder head temperatures stay within limits.

If you leave the throttle at the initial cruise setting as fuel is consumed and weight is reduced, you will notice an increase in true airspeed. Why not tweak the throttle back to maintain the planned airspeed and conserve some fuel? At this point, fuel conservation (which translates into more time in the air) takes precedence over having the throttle fully open.

You may be working on your multiengine rating in an airplane with auxiliary or tip tanks, and this will help you to prepare for the fuel

		STANDARD TEMPERATURE 3° C		
RPM	MP	% BHP	KTAS	GPH
2500	30	81	132	17.8
	28	75	127	16.4
	26	69	122	15.1
	24	63	116	13.8
	22	56	109	12.4
2400	30	76	128	16.6
	28	71	123	15.4
	26	65	118	14.2
	24	59	112	13.0
	22	53	105	11.8
2300	30	73	125	15.9
	28	68	121	14.8
	26	62	115	13.7
	24	56	109	12.5
	22	50	102	11.3
2200	30	69	122	15.1
	28	64	117	14.0
	26	58	111	12.9
	24	53	111	11.8
	22	47	98	10.7
FOR EDUCATIONAL USE ONLY NOT FOR OPERATION OF ANY AIRCRAFT				

Figure 6-2. Cruise power chart

systems in more sophisticated aircraft. If this is the case, you may be tempted to use all of the fuel in the auxiliary tanks during cruise. Don't do it. When you allow the fuel lines to fill with air, you deprive the fuel pumps of their ability to work for you. They are not designed to move air. It can take an uncomfortably long time to restart a fuel-injected engine that has been deprived of fuel, but that's not the only drawback. You lose the advantage of dual systems while the dry engine is sucking frantically for some liquid refreshment, and, if you are drawing a heavy load from both alternators or running the de-icing boots with the vacuum pumps, purposely failing an engine may create more problems than you can easily handle.

Engine Failure During Cruise Flight

The sudden cessation of sound from one side of the fuselage is never welcome, but if it has to happen, let it be in cruise. With a comfortable quantity of air between the airplane and the ground, an engine failure should be more of an inconvenience than an emergency. Unfortunately, National Transportation Safety Board (NTSB) statistics indicate that most accidents involving multiengine aircraft begin during the cruising phase. This does not imply that the airplanes fell from the sky like dead ducks, but that the loss (or partial loss) of an engine at altitude began a series of pilot errors or misjudgments that culminated in a mishap. Of course, there are no NTSB statistics on how many twins experienced some sort of problem during cruise and landed without incident.

The reason that, despite statistics, you would rather have a power loss at altitude rather than during takeoff or approach is that altitude gives you the luxury of time. At 10,000 feet above the terrain, with the airplane under control and trimmed for hands-off flight, you can reach into the back seat for the Pilot's Operating Handbook and read the emergency procedure section in detail.

Unless you have had a catastrophic failure, such as losing part of a propeller blade or blowing a cylinder through the nacelle, you will have time to experiment with sources of fuel and ignition in an attempt to regain full or partial power. Most total power losses are fuel related, either fuel starvation, caused by mismanagement of the fuel on board, or fuel exhaustion, caused by poor planning on the part of the hapless pilot.

There is no question that any unusual noise or vibration during what should be the most relaxed portion of the flight can be unsettling, and that in the event of an actual power loss, there will be some delay in reacting caused by the "This can't be happening to me!" syndrome.

At the instant of failure, the airplane will lurch toward the ailing engine, the propellers will go out of synchronization, and the passengers will start peppering you with questions. However, the airplane will not immediately roll over on its back and dive for the ground as television viewing might lead you to expect. You will be able to establish lateral control easily, because aileron control will be very effective at cruise speeds. Heading control is another matter. The plane will want to yaw toward the sick engine, and full rudder-pedal deflection may be required until you can get the rudder trim to help out. The airplane will not lose altitude solely because of the engine problem; in fact, you may be able to convert excess airspeed into a shallow (and momentary) climb.

Trim for hands-off flight and start looking for reasons that the engine quit (I am assuming a non-catastrophic failure). Fuel flow OK? Is the answer as simple as throwing a fuel pump switch or moving a fuel selector? If that's the answer, hold on a minute — pull the throttle back near idle before you force feed the engine with a big gulp of fuel and cause a power surge. If fuel is available to the engine, could the problem be ignition? Try operating on each magneto individually. If one mag has jumped out of time, the engine may run perfectly well on the other one. Again, to avoid backfiring, reduce the throttle setting before you experiment with the magnetos . If there is fuel and ignition, is the engine having trouble breathing? Could the air intake be blocked by ice, wet snow, or some failure in the plumbing? Try the alternate air source, which bypasses the normal air intake. Will the engine run at a lower power setting? Try adjusting the mixture. If the engine is getting too much air because of a leak in the intake manifold, you may be able to re-establish a viable fuel-air ratio.

Drift Down

What is the single-engine service ceiling for your airplane? It is the altitude at which the airplane has essentially lost all climb capability. The official definition is a climb rate of 50 feet-per-minute, but that minuscule rate will be erased by control movement in reaction to even light turbulence. It's a good number to keep in mind, though, especially if you are flying in mountainous terrain. Let's assume the worst: you have tried all of the suggested methods above and nothing has worked. Both magnetos are out to lunch, or there is a blockage that keeps fuel from the engine. You have, reluctantly but calmly, feathered the propeller of the offending engine and completed the shutdown checklist. What now? If the failure occurred above the single-engine service ceiling, not much. If you trim to maintain blue line airspeed, the airplane will lose altitude very slowly as it drifts down toward the service ceiling, and it will cover a lot of ground while doing so. When the single-engine service ceiling is reached, of course, the airplane will stop losing altitude. Don't consider this as a means of making it to your destination on one engine. Use the drift down capability as a means of getting to a suitable airport.

CHAPTER SEVEN

DESCENT, APPROACH AND LANDING

DESCENT PLANNING

ALTHOUGH YOU RAN THROUGH THE TIME, FUEL and distance-to-descend calculations as a part of preflight planning, as you near the destination conditions will probably be different than anticipated.

Under instrument flight rules, some descent decisions are forced on you by air traffic control, and you must make the best of them. However, a little judicious bugging of the air traffic controller might get you "expect lower in ten miles" or something similar, giving you time to make preparations. Your goal is to establish a comfortable descent rate at cruise speed without extreme power changes. You should know how many minutes you are from the destination by reference to the DME, the Loran, or through exercising your pilotage navigation skills; allow 3 minutes per 1000 feet of altitude loss. Your passengers will appreciate a 300-foot per-minute descent.

Beginning the Descent

Earlier, I recommended a "one size fits all" propeller setting of 2,300 RPM during cruising flight, with manifold pressure set by the book to provide 65 to 70 percent power and the mixture set 50 degrees on the rich side of peak EGT. The first step in preparing to descend is a reduction in prop speed to the bottom of the governing range — this should be about 2,000 to 2,100 RPM. Note that this is my recommendation; the engine manufacturers suggest an initial throttle reduction. I use this method and it works. If you are cruising at 14,000 feet and the manifold pressure has fallen to 20 inches at full throttle, pulling the props back from 2,300 to 2,000 RPM will bring the pressures up no more than three inches; pull the throttles back to their cruise setting. You should now be showing 20 inches and 2,000 RPM and descending at a comfortable rate.

The situation you want to avoid is high prop

speed and low manifold pressure. This is what Lycoming says on the subject in the Lycoming Flyer: "Unless the pilot takes certain precautions, fast descents carrying high cruise RPM and low manifold pressure cause broken piston rings from ring flutter, and also cause cracked cylinders at the spark plug and valve ports, and warped exhaust valves due to sudden cooling . . . we recommend that the pilot maintain at least 15 inches MP or higher with pressurized aircraft and set the RPM at the lowest cruise setting . . ."

Reducing prop RPM will increase the load on the propeller and keep the engine working so that it will stay toasty warm on the way down. As manifold pressure increases in the descent, reduce the setting to keep manifold pressure at the cruise setting. Leave the mixtures alone. I know, I know, most handbooks tell you to go to full rich when descending, but think of the effect on the engines of suddenly increasing the percentage of fuel in the mixture.

Remember that the fuel in the tanks has been subjected to some fairly cold temperatures for a long period of time, and that little warming will occur as it makes its way through the fuel selector and pumps. RAM Aircraft Corporation, a major overhauler and modifier, says, "The rich mixture manifests itself as a lot of cold fuel entering a hot cylinder intake air port at the fuel injection nozzle outlet. The conditions for 'shock' cooling have been met . . ." Your goal should be to keep the engines warm, so don't go for the mixture knobs until the engines tell you that they are beginning to run lean. Try to keep the exhaust gas temperature 50 degrees cooler than the peak temperature you used for cruise. Believe me, if the engines don't like what you are doing, they will let you know by running rough, and your reaction should be to richen only enough to make them run smoothly again. RAM says that you should not go to full rich until you are on the runway with engines at idle. A check of the exhaust gas and cylinder head temperatures should show that leaving the mixture untouched has kept the cylinder head temperature in the middle of the green and the exhaust gas temperature about two-thirds of the way to peak.

Leveling Off

Within the gradual-power-reduction guidelines mentioned earlier, keep the manifold pressure close to what it was in cruise (because MAP increases 1 inch per 1,000 feet of descent, this will require a reduction of about 1 inch every 2 minutes). When you have descended to pattern altitude or initial approach altitude, put the props back at 2,300 RPM and leave them there until the wheels are on the runway; 17 inches should result in approach speed. That raises another point: prop pitch changes make noise, and pitch changes at low altitude cause people on the ground to reach for their binoculars with one hand and their telephone with the other hand. If you push the prop controls full forward because of a possible go-around, make sure that the final RPM change is made after the governors have driven the propeller blades to their flattest pitch.

Remember when zero thrust was discussed? The zero-thrust power setting is used in training to simulate an engine-out situation while keeping the engine available for use. When the manifold pressure is higher than the zero-thrust setting, the propeller is pulling the airplane forward through the air, and the bearings and seals in the drive train are experiencing the loads that they were designed to handle. At power settings below zero thrust, however, the airplane is moving through the air faster than the propeller can turn, causing the propeller to drive the engine. That reverses the loads on the seals

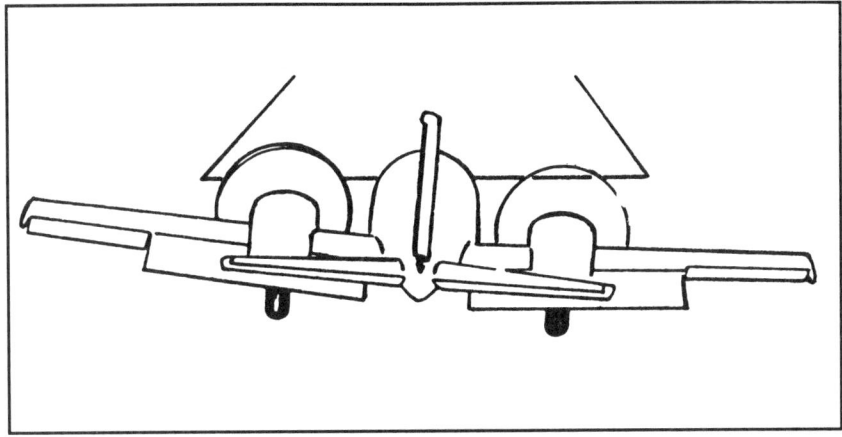

Figure 7-1. Flat-plate drag

and bearings, which is not good, and also creates a tremendous amount of drag. That drag is called flat-plate drag, because the effect is the same as if a 72-inch or 84-inch (depending on propeller blade length) flat plate is attached to the crankshaft. Retarding the throttles past the zero-thrust setting places the propellers in the flat-plate drag range, and, accordingly, you should avoid power settings below 12 inches.

Flat-plate drag can be a useful tool if used wisely. If you have allowed the engines to cool gradually and find that you need to lose some altitude, pulling the throttles back to the stops will cause the airplane to sink dramatically. Leaving them there, however, can result in a hard landing. Two (imaginary) flat plates attached to the nacelles mean disturbed airflow over the horizontal stabilizer, and reduced elevator authority. You might attempt to flare and find out too late that back pressure on the yoke has no effect. Never be in the flat-plate drag/manifold pressure range on short final.

On Final

When you make your first landing in a twin, it will be apparent that you will be seeing things differently than you did in a single-engine airplane; there won't be an engine cowling to obscure a portion of the approach path. Instead of eyeballing the descent path, you will use a combination of airplane configuration and attitude control (as reflected by airspeed). Flying by the numbers is the only way to land a multi-engine airplane.

The manufacturer provides a landing configuration and airspeed in the Pilot's Operating Handbook; the recommended airspeed may vary with your airplane's landing weight. When you extend landing flaps and maintain the suggested airspeed, the resulting pitch attitude insures that you will land on the main wheels. Watch an air carrier jet land and transfer that mental picture into your twin. The pilot of that jet configures the airplane for landing several miles from the touchdown point and maintains a reference speed all the way to touchdown. "Ref," as it is called, is based on landing weight and stall speed, and the captain flies a profile based on the reference speed. It might call for ref plus 20 knots until intercepting the final approach course, ref plus 10 to the final approach fix, and ref plus no more than 5 knots on final. Because flight at reference speed in the landing configuration results in a slightly nose-high attitude, little or no flare is used — they just fly it onto the runway.

Your propeller twin will deliver the best results if you fly it just as an airline captain flies a jet, making speed control paramount. Because the reference speed typically allows only a 20 percent cushion over the stall, you may add a correction factor for gusting crosswinds, such as all of the steady state headwind component plus one-half of the gusts. This is intended to keep a

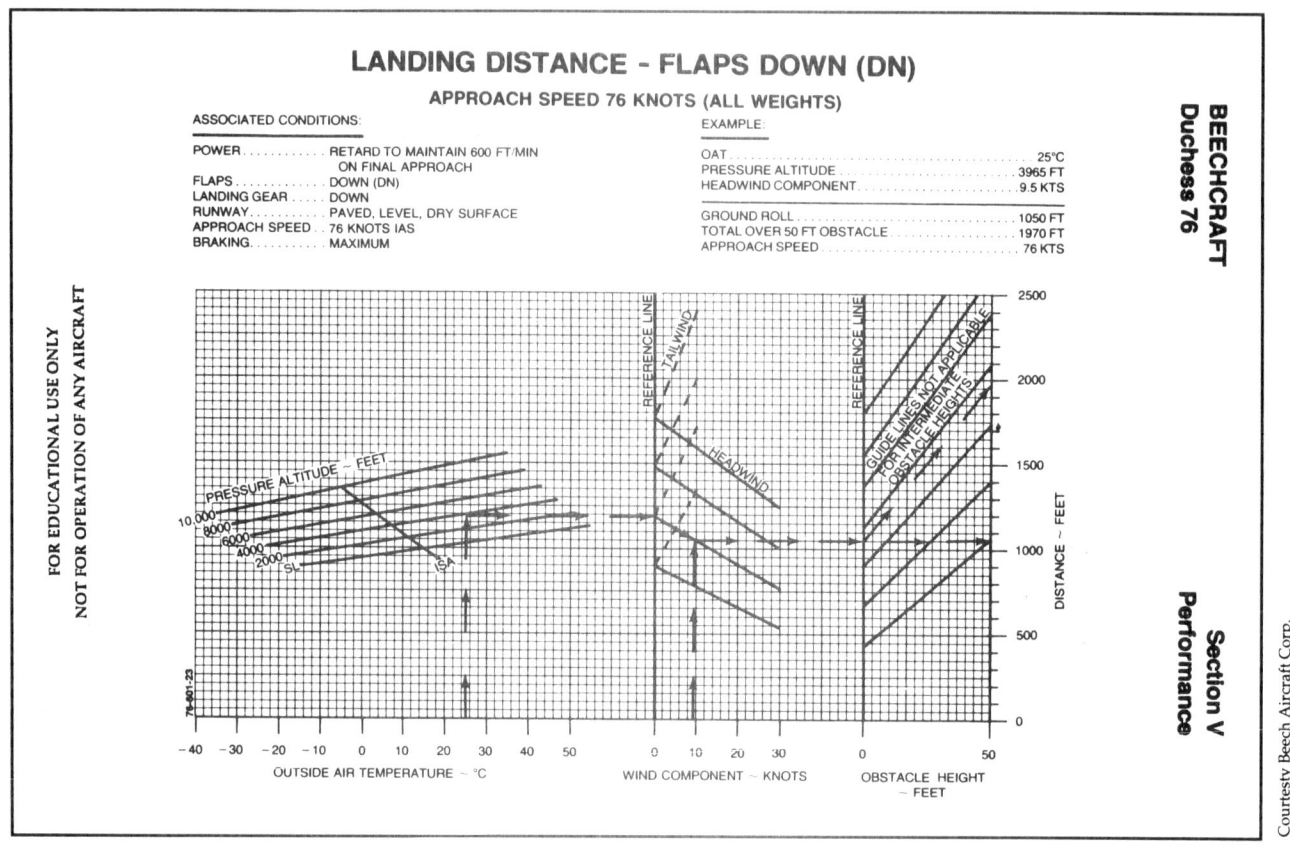

Figure 7-2. Landing distance

sudden lull in the wind from dropping the airplane onto the runway.

Landing Distance

In the case of the Duchess, figure 7-2 indicates a recommended approach speed of 76 knots and 600 feet per minute with full flaps. Note that the charted landing distances are achieved with maximum braking, a method you will probably not use. Also, if there is a 50-foot obstacle right at the threshold, you will land at least 633 feet down the runway after barely clearing it. Under the conditions in the sample problem, much warmer than standard temperature at a pressure altitude of almost 4,000 feet, the ground roll begins 920 feet beyond the obstacle.

Those are all of the elements involved in multiengine descent planning. A thorough, conservative pilot will go through all of the planning steps before each trip.

Getting It Stopped

As the pilot of a multiengine airplane, you must remember that getting it stopped on the ground is a question of energy management, and that you must reduce the total energy to virtually zero before you will be able to turn off at an intersection. The amount of energy under your control is a combination of weight and airspeed.

When you are loading and fueling the airplane before departure, landing distance at the destination may not have a very high priority; when you are on short final, however, you may wish that you didn't have quite so many pounds to bring to a halt. You already know the importance of a low touchdown speed; the energy present when the rubber meets the runway must be dissipated by friction, either the rolling friction of the tires on the runway or the use of brakes. Unless you are landing at Cape Canaveral, rolling to a stop is impractical. Aerodynamic drag is a function of the square of the airspeed, and once the airplane has slowed to 60 or 70 percent of touchdown speed, that source of drag is pretty useless. The flaps played their role when you established the landing configuration, by permitting a lower approach speed, and once you are on the runway they are out of the picture.

The smartest action you can take is to get on the brakes just as soon as the full weight of the airplane is on the tires. It takes just as much braking energy to slow from 85 knots to 65 knots, early in the landing roll, as it does to decelerate from 55 knots to 7 knots as you approach the end of the runway — you are not saving the brakes by waiting. The brakes are most effective if you retract the flaps, transferring any weight still being carried by the wings to the landing gear. I know all of the arguments against going for the flap handle before turning off the runway for fear of retracting the gear by mistake, but you must balance that risk against the importance of a short landing roll. Don't shrug off a slight tailwind; when the tailwind component is 5 percent of touchdown speed, the ground roll will be 50 percent longer than it would be if you were landing into the same wind.

Multiengine flying and instrument weather go together, and you must consider the effect that a wet or slippery runway will have on the rollout. Remember that the maximum speed to avoid hydroplaning is 9 times the square root of the tire pressure. Beechcraft recommends that Duchess tires be inflated to 38 pounds, which suggests the danger of hydroplaning at speeds higher than 57 knots. That's the kind of calculation you can make well before takeoff.

Single-Engine Approach and Landing

According to the National Transportation Safety Board, most fatal twin accidents occur during the approach and landing after losing an engine during cruise or descent, yet during your multiengine training you will land time after time with one engine operating properly and the other one operating at or close to zero thrust.

Figure 7-3. Engine-out landing

This would suggest either that pilots landing with an engine feathered are making poor decisions at critical times or that the apparent ease of single-engine approaches during training has not prepared them for the real thing. One possibility is that the pilots are getting low and slow and forgetting that punching up the power on the operating engine causes both roll and yaw problems. You should prepare for that eventuality by deciding that you will never let the airspeed deteriorate below the blue line and that you will always be a little high on final. A dot above the glideslope or white over pink on the Visual Approach Slope Indicator is sufficiently high. This may result in a longer landing than you would like, but as I mentioned when discussing engine loss immediately after takeoff, it is better to slide off the end of the runway at 40 knots than to fall out of the sky.

Another possible reason that pilots lose control on final approach is cascading problems; because of the engine failure, some aircraft system doesn't work and the pilot becomes overloaded. A typical scenario might find a pilot flying on one engine and unable to extend the landing

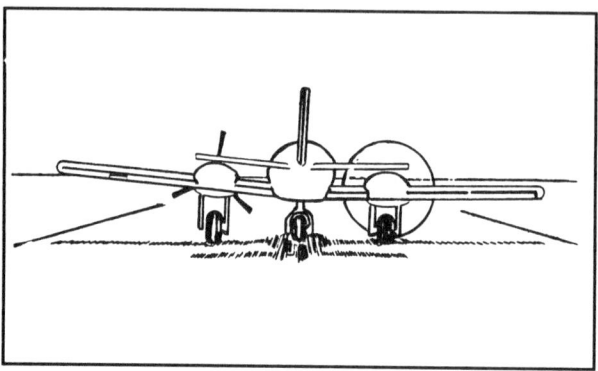

Figure 7-4. Landing with a propeller feathered

gear. Departing the airport area while extending the gear by emergency means is the wrong answer. The airplane probably won't maintain altitude on one engine with the gear down, so the pilot gets the gear down but can't make it back to the airport. Remember that an aircraft in distress has priority; if you have to, don't hesitate to tie up the whole airport area while you get your problem solved.

When should the wheels be lowered for landing if one prop has been feathered? At the point where you normally begin the descent to land. If the extension system is not going to work, you need to find that out while you have plenty of altitude. Don't let the drag of the gear take you below the glideslope or, in level flight, cause the airspeed to fall below the blue line. *NEVER LET THE SPEED GET BELOW VYSE.* If you can't maintain altitude without slowing below blue line airspeed, put the wheels back in the wells until you need to extend them for landing. It's better to land with the gear up than to lose control because of limited engine-out performance.

A go-around on one engine in a light to medium twin is something that is taught, practiced, and written about, but is seldom successful under actual conditions. Remember that a light twin does not have to demonstrate a positive climb capability on one engine, and that the FAA does not even require that an applicant for the multiengine rating demonstrate the ability to wave off on one engine. Do not consider a single-engine go-around as a viable option unless you make the decision with airspeed and altitude to spare. When you have descended to less than 500 feet above the ground, you should consider yourself committed to land. Les Berven, the FAA's guru for single-engine flight, says that he would not attempt a single-engine go-around in anything smaller than a King Air.

Landing with a Propeller Feathered

Landing with a propeller feathered is one thing you will probably never practice, so your first such landing will be cold turkey. When you reduce power to flare, the airplane will want to turn toward the good engine (in no-wind conditions), because of the drag of the windmilling propeller and the fact that there is absolutely no drag on the failed engine side. Expect to float farther than normal because of the reduced drag. Once the airplane has touched down, the wing on the side with the feathered propeller will tend to lift, again because it is relatively clean aerodynamically in comparison to the good engine side (figure 7-4). For that reason, the tire on that side will have less weight on it. If you treat the situation normally and apply even braking, the airplane will swerve toward the good engine side and possibly blow a tire. Use intermittent light braking on the failed engine side until the weight rests solidly on both wheels. Wind from the good engine side will make things worse, while a wind from the failed engine side will help. And you will be in no position to shop around for runways with favorable winds.

Taxiing with an engine feathered is another challenge, because the airplane will refuse to turn toward the good engine. Expect a series of 270-degree turns toward the dead engine as you make your way to the ramp. If taxiing is difficult, don't abuse the remaining engine by pulling lots of power with little cooling. Get the airplane off the runway and call for help.

CHAPTER EIGHT

PREPARING FOR THE CHECKRIDE

ASSUMING THAT YOU ARE ADDING THE MULTI-engine rating to your private pilot certificate, your examiner will be using the Practical Test Standards for that rating during your checkride. Because a few pilots do get their original Private tickets in twins (the late Danny Kaye, for instance), the test standards include several tasks which you completed for your single engine rating. Don't worry — your MEL checkride will not duplicate any of those tasks (see Appendix I).

If you are reading this as a certificated Commercial pilot who is adding the Multiengine rating, you will find that the Commercial checkride duplicates the Private ride almost exactly, except for the stalls. The major difference is that each task includes the following as an Objective: "Exhibits commercial pilot knowledge by explaining...," whereas the Private pilot must only "exhibit knowledge." After reading this book, a Commercial certificate applicant will be able to satisfy an examiner as to his or her "Commercial pilot knowledge," and a Private pilot applying for a Multiengine certificate will have no trouble with the oral.

Certificates and Documents

Be prepared to show the examiner not only the airframe log but *two* engine logs. In addition to showing the examiner that the airplane is not out of a 100-hour inspection or an annual, check the time on the propellers. They, too, must be inspected at regular intervals that do not always coincide with airframe inspection times.

Become familiar with the weight-and-balance records and find the most recent Form 337. When you are asked to perform a weight-and-balance calculation, you must use the most current information. If you intend to fly the airplane on instruments after you pass the checkride, this would also be a good time to determine how recently the pitot-static and transponder inspections were performed.

Airplane Systems

The examiner will ask you to explain how the flight controls are actuated, the power source of each flight instrument, and how the landing gear is extended, both normally and in an emergency. You will be asked how the propeller

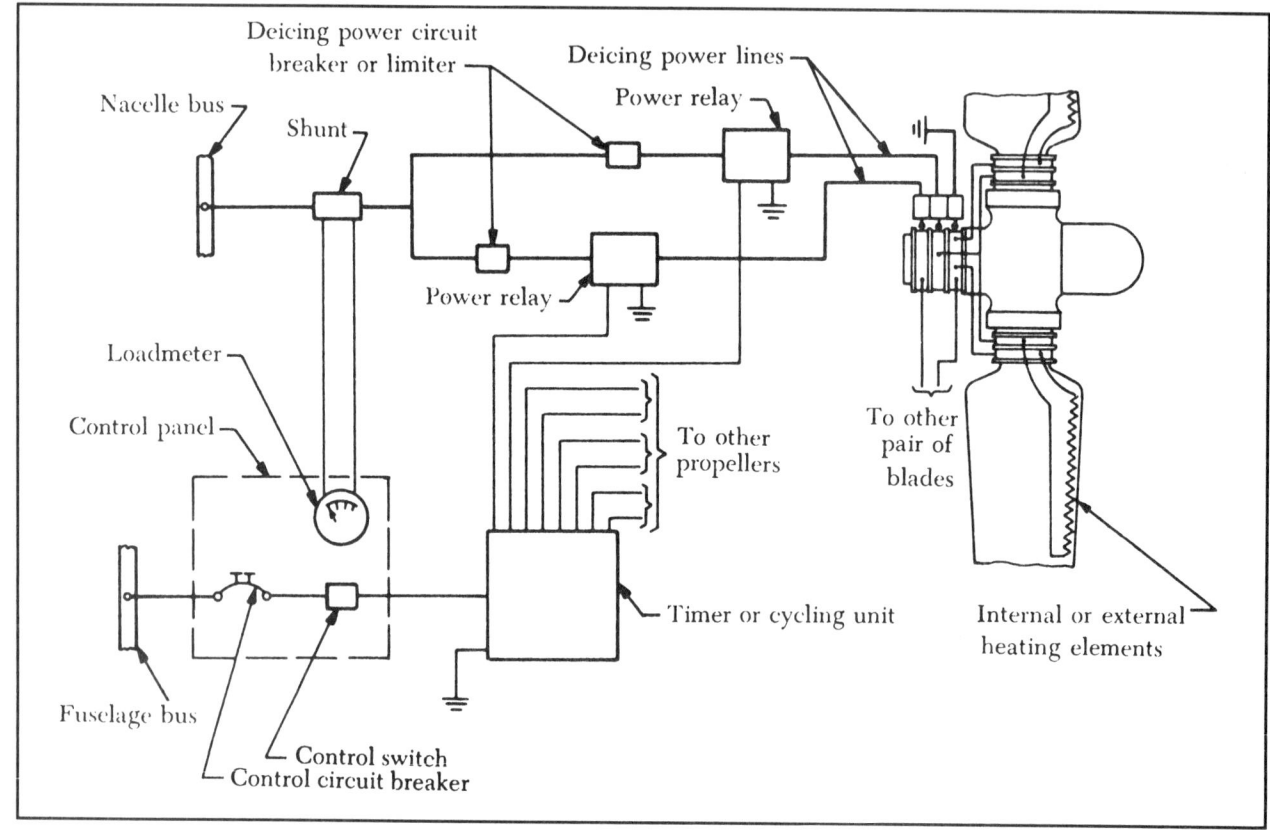

Figure 8-1. Typical engine de-icing system

blade angle is changed and the effect of problems with the governor. You should be able to explain the fuel system and tell the examiner how you would ensure continued fuel flow to an engine if a particular pump or valve failed.

The same types of questions will be asked about the electrical system: If you lose part of your electrical supply, how will you cope with the loss? If your airplane is equipped with de-ice and/or anti-ice, be prepared to tell the examiner how the system works. Know how the environmental system works. Where is the heater safety switch? Can you warm up the passengers without toasting the cockpit crew? Can you operate the windshield defroster without frosting the passengers?

Normal Procedures

Be able to name every V-speed applicable to the test airplane and tell the examiner when each speed is appropriate. Know the various limiting weights. If you take off at maximum gross takeoff weight and lose an engine, will the airplane be at or below its maximum gross landing weight if you try a turn back to the runway? Are there any other limitations (zero-fuel weight, prop RPM caution arcs, etc.) that apply? If there are any placards or limiting markings, be ready to tell the examiner why they are there and what might happen if you ignored them. Do you know how to start an engine using external power, without frying the electrical system?

Determining Performance and Flight Planning

You should be able to use every chart and graph in the performance section of the Pilot's Operating Handbook. Prepare for the checkride by planning imaginary trips and calculating takeoff distances, fuel burn to altitude, landing distance, and other relevant factors.

Do some weight-and-balance problems that

involve shifting passengers between seats (or removing weight) to place the center of gravity within limits. Your twin gives you more loading flexibility as well as more opportunities to load the airplane improperly.

Minimum Equipment List

Your light twin is subject to FAR 91.30 (Inoperable instruments and equipment) and its requirement that all installed equipment must be operative or the airplane is considered unairworthy. There may be a Master Minimum Equipment List (MMEL) for your airplane that designates some pieces of equipment as not required for flight; if that is the case, have a copy of the MMEL and any supporting documents available to show to the examiner.

It may be that some pieces of installed equipment can be placarded as inoperative and the airplane determined to be airworthy without that equipment. Know which items, if any, can be so designated. The key is to show the examiner that you are aware of the requirement for Minimum Equipment Lists, how your operation is affected, and that you know how to work around the restrictions if allowed to do so by 91.30.

Flight Principles — Engine Inoperative

The examiner will ask you to explain the effect on single-engine flight of density altitude and airplane loading. You will be asked to explain the term "critical engine" and tell the examiner which engine is critical (if any) on your airplane. Be prepared to explain Vmc, how it is determined, and its relationship to indicated stall speed and altitude. You should be ready to discuss takeoff planning from determining safe runway length to single-engine climb gradient after takeoff.

Ground Operations

Carry a checklist in your hand while doing the preflight walkaround. Know exactly how many fuel drains there are and which sump or filter each one serves. Be able to explain each and every knob and switch in the cockpit. Although your instructor may not let you use the autopilot during training, the examiner expects you to know how to use it and, most important, how to disengage it in case of a malfunction. The same is true of oxygen systems.

Don't forget to check that the door is closed properly and that the examiner has both seat belt and shoulder harness fastened. Brief the examiner on how to open the seat belt and door if you are disabled — remember that the examiner is playing the role of a passenger.

Use a checklist during engine start and the preflight runup. The FAA encourages checklist use and the examiner will look for it. Be ready to explain why you perform runup actions, such as the alternator check, exercising the propeller, and the feather check.

Normal and Crosswind Takeoffs and Climbs

Refer to the Normal Takeoff Distance chart in the performance section and follow the procedure and airspeed listed there. It will probably recommend standing on the brakes and running the throttles up to takeoff power. If no liftoff speed is listed, rotate at Vmc plus 5 knots. Climb at Vy (not Vyse) plus or minus 5 knots to a safe maneuvering altitude before the first power reduction.

The examiner may fail an engine before you reach liftoff speed — be ready to chop the throttles and get on the brakes. Know your crosswind takeoff procedure, and remember that a little additional throttle on the upwind engine can help offset a crosswind.

Maximum Performance Takeoffs and Climb

Again, check the charts in the performance section and fly the airplane using the procedure shown. You should definitely stand on the brakes and apply full power for an obstacle-clearance takeoff, and rotate at the recommended speed. The only difference from a

normal takeoff is the initial climb speed of Vx until the obstacle is cleared.

Instrument Flight

If you hold an Instrument rating on your Single-engine certificate, you will be required to demonstrate your ability to handle engine-out emergencies under simulated instrument conditions and to perform instrument approach procedures with one engine inoperative.

A proficient instrument pilot should have no trouble meeting these requirements. You will be amply warned when the examiner simulates engine failure, because the props will go out of sync and the airplane will lurch toward the failed engine. The ball will deflect toward the good engine. You must fix your eyes on the flight instruments and maintain heading with rudder pressure. That pressure will help you identify the failed engine, and you can then go through the verification and feathering procedure by feel, keeping your eyes fixed on the flight instruments.

Note that the Practical Test Standards call for securing the engine before attempting to determine the reason for the failure. And if the examiner fails an engine while you are in a turn, you will find it easier to identify the failed engine if you roll out of the bank.

Remember that a bank toward the good engine is required to maintain a heading. If you level the wings during an instrument approach, the good engine will drive you off of the final approach course. This is the most difficult aspect of a single-engine ILS; if you relax the bank, you will lose the localizer.

Flight at Critically Slow Airspeed

You will be expected to confidently and competently maneuver the airplane at speeds as slow as 10 knots above stall speed (or Vmc, whichever is greater) plus or minus 5 knots, in a variety of gear and flap configurations dictated by the examiner. Slow flight is an excellent confidence builder. At least one training session should be devoted exclusively to exploring the low speed end of the airplane's operating envelope.

If you are a Private pilot who is upgrading to twins, you will be expected to demonstate entries to and recoveries from imminent stalls. The Practical Test Standard goes so far as to say "avoid full stalls." However, if you are going for Commercial privileges, full stalls are required. Figure that one out.

Remember that full stalls are hard on airplanes, because the rotating propellers are excellent gyroscopes. A rapid pitching moment, such as you may use in a stall recovery, will exert lateral bending forces on the crankshaft extensions to which the propeller is attached.

No matter which rating you are being tested for, you will be expected to recover to level flight by smoothly reducing the angle of attack, adding power to minimize altitude loss, and retracting the gear and flaps if they were extended.

Constant-Altitude Turns

You will be asked to perform a 40-to-50 degree banked 360-degree turn while maintaining altitude, and rolling out within 10 degrees of the entry heading. With this degree of bank, both load factor and induced drag increase, and extra power may be required to maintain altitude. Be sure you know what the maneuvering speed is for your twin, and don't begin the steep turn at a speed higher than Va. Expect the overbanking tendency to be more noticeable than it was in single-engine airplanes.

SYSTEM AND EQUIPMENT MALFUNCTIONS

This is an inflight extension of your explanation of the airplane systems in that the examiner will simulate failure of a system to observe how you respond. Fortunately for you, there is no way that the examiner can set an engine on fire, cause a loss of oil pressure, or dump the hydraulic fluid. However, examiners can do just about everything else. Expect one landing without operative pitch trim and another without flaps, and don't be surprised if a door pops open during a takeoff. The examiner needs to evaluate not only your knowledge of the airplane's systems, but how you react to unfamiliar situations. An imaginative instructor can do a lot to prepare you for this part of the checkride, but you can do a lot for yourself by sitting down with the manual and playing "what if?"

Maneuvering with One Engine Inoperative

This should be easy, because your instructor will be pulling engines throughout your training. The examiner will want to see how you react to an in-flight failure, and if you can perform normal flight maneuvers with an engine out. You will be expected to maintain heading and altitude in straight-and-level flight, climb and descend to assigned altitudes, and perform turns both toward and away from the dead engine. Your mind will be on the failed engine and the control problems it will cause, and it will be easy to let the heading or altitude slip a little. Don't let it happen.

There is no airspeed standard other than "Attains the best engine-inoperative airspeed" listed under Objectives. In level flight, a high airspeed suggests that the good engine is being overworked, while a speed below Vyse is unacceptable. You won't find a recommended engine-out cruise speed in the performance charts. I suggest Vyse plus 10 knots. You should be able to attain that speed without beating up on the good engine, affording an airspeed cushion for turbulence and maneuvering. If your instructor knows that your type of twin operates best at a certain speed, by all means go with his or her experience.

When the examiner fails an engine, by whatever means, identify the failed engine and then go through your troubleshooting routine before feathering the propeller on the offending engine. Because an in-flight restart may be part of this Task, don't be surprised if the examiner lets you go all the way to feather. Don't look over at the examiner and say "Do you want me to feather it?" If going to full feather is not on the examiner's agenda, he will keep the prop control out of the feather detent with a strategically placed thumb on the quadrant, or by quickly moving the prop control back to high pitch.

It won't take much effort to turn toward the dead engine, because the good engine has been waiting for you to give it an opportunity to take charge of directional control. Watch out for overbanking. On the other hand, banking toward the good engine will require more aileron deflection than usual. I am assuming that you already have the rudder trim set toward the good engine side to give your leg a rest.

If the examiner allows you to feather the propeller and then demonstrate an air start, be sure to use the restart checklist, and expect the engine to be hard to start. Remember that cooling air has been passing through the nacelle at 100 knots or so for the past few minutes and that the fuel-air mixture will be reluctant to vaporize in that chilly environment.

Engine Inoperative, Loss of Directional Control Demonstration

The Vmc demonstration in a multiengine airplane is similar to the stall series you performed on your private pilot checkride. You are showing the examiner that you know what to do if you get the airplane into a situation it should never be in.

The examiner will have determined that you know the relationship between indicated stall speed and Vmc, and you should agree on an altitude for the demonstration which is low enough to allow the aiplane to reach Vmc before it stalls and yet high enough for safety.

Just as was the case with departure stalls and approach stalls, a certain amount of stage setting is required. Because the Vmc demo is supposed to duplicate an immediately after-takeoff situation, the gear should be up and the flaps should be in the takeoff position. The engines should be set at their rated takeoff power. The examiner will reduce one engine to idle while you establish a single-engine climb attitude at Vyse and then, while banking into the good engine and maintaining heading with rudder, increase the angle of attack until you run out of rudder or lose directional control. As soon as either of these conditions is met, the examiner will expect you to reduce the angle of attack and simultaneously reduce the power on the operating engine. You aren't expected to chop the throttle completely — just reduce power enough to regain control with a minimum loss of altitude.

Because full rudder deflection is a measure of minimum control speed (with the pedal against the metal, haven't you lost the ability to exert control? The airplane doesn't have to get away from you to demonstrate Vmc), many instructors and examiners will sacrifice their toes and shoeshines by sticking a foot under the rudder pedal on the good engine side.

By the way, as a single-engine pilot you are expected to practice stalls occasionally, and you might want to do it solo. As a multiengine pilot, you should never practice Vmc without a qualified pilot in the right seat.

Demonstrating the Effects of Various Airspeeds and Configurations During Engine-Inoperative Performance

The drag demonstration is intended to show the examiner that you understand how aircraft configuration affects performance under engine-out conditions and, accordingly, that you will establish a minimum-drag configuration in the event of engine failure.

The examiner will ask you to establish the airplane in level flight at Vyse, with the critical engine at zero thrust. You will first demonstrate the importance of maintaining single-engine best rate-of-climb speed by varying the airspeed and noting that performance deteriorates at speeds faster or slower than Vyse. While maintaining blue line airspeed, you will first extend the gear, then the flaps, and then both gear and flaps, while recording the rate of descent caused by the drag of each item. Finally, you will move the propellor control into flat pitch (high RPM) and record the resulting rate of descent. You should allow 3 minutes in each configuration so that the descent rates can stabilize.

Engine Failure Enroute

The examiner may combine this task with MANEUVERING WITH ONE ENGINE INOPERATIVE. There is no difference in your required actions, except that you will be expected to establish a minimum sink rate (drift down). Use Vyse if the airplane manual does not specify an airspeed.

Engine Failure on Takeoff Before VMC

This is easy, because you should be spring-loaded to reduce the throttles to idle and get on the brakes if ANYTHING unusual happens before the airspeed needle reaches the red line.

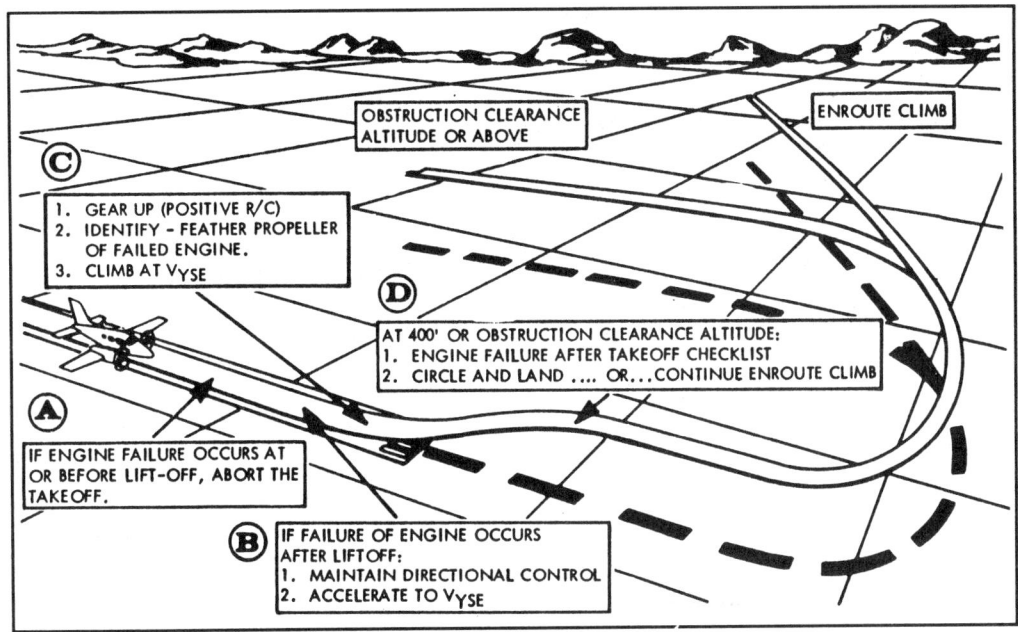

Figure 8-2. Engine failure during takeoff procedures

Engine Failure After Liftoff

The examiner will expect you to ensure that all of the engine controls are set at full power and that drag items have been cleaned up before you identify, verify, and feather. With the airplane under control, use the checklist to secure the failed engine. Don't go through your troubleshooting routine until the airplane has reached a safe altitude.

Approach and Landing with an Inoperative Engine

If the examiner fails an engine after you have reduced power to initiate the descent for landing, you may have to add power to get enough differential rudder pressure to identify the dead engine. Don't let the confusion of the moment make you forget the Prelanding Checklist. Airspeed should be within plus 5 knots of the blue line. Don't let the airspeed get below the blue line. Use power on the good engine to maintain a stabilized descent rate, and be alert on the rudders as you reduce power to land. Keep the airplane aligned with the runway.

Landing with "zero thrust" on one engine does not prepare you for landing with an engine feathered, because the manufacturer's zero thrust settings are based on flight at Vyse. Those settings will result in some drag as speed is reduced in the flare for landing. In contrast, a feathered propeller would create no drag.

You can add a little realism to your engine-out landing practice (without shaking up the tower controllers by landing with one prop standing still) by calculating a touchdown-zero-thrust setting. First determine the ratio between Vyse and touchdown speed. If blue line is 87 and you normally touch down at 70, the ratio is 70/87 or 0.8. Then fly at Vyse using 12 inches (or the manufacturer's recommended manifold pressure for zero thrust), push the prop control full forward, and note the resulting RPM; let's say that it is 2,300 RPM. Multiply 2,300 by .8 to get 1,840. The next time you flare for touchdown with a simulated engine out, adjust the RPM to 1,840 with the throttle (the propeller pitch will be as flat as it can get, the governor will have lost control, and you will be able to control RPM with the throttle).

Balked Landing

The FAA does not require that you demonstrate the ability to execute a missed approach on one

Figure 8-3. Feathered propeller reduces drag

engine. However, you are expected to demonstrate to the examiner that you can recognize a bad landing approach and go around for another try. The examiner will be watching to see how you handle the gear, the flaps, and the cowl flaps (if installed) and to see if you use a checklist to ensure that you didn't miss anything. Climb out at Vy plus or minus 5 knots.

Normal and Crosswind Approaches and Landings

Know the demonstrated maximum crosswind for your airplane and, if there is no crosswind, be ready to explain crosswind landing procedure to the examiner. The examiner will be looking for a constant approach speed and a constant descent path. Whether or not that means a constant rate of descent depends on the wind. Expect to make small pitch and power adjustments all the way down the descent path. Maintain the indicated airspeed within plus or minus 5 knots of the recommended approach speed. Check the landing distance graphs in the Performance section of the operating handbook for the speed. Make sure that you don't reduce the throttle below about 12 inches to avoid getting into the flat-plate drag range.

Maximum Performance Approach and Landing

Refer to the charts in the Performance section of the operating handbook for the airspeed and flap setting to use for a short field landing. You will learn more from the performance charts than you will from reading the Normal Procedures section. Don't let your desire to land short fool you into pulling the throttles back to idle at the low airspeeds recommended for maximum performance landings.

With reduced airflow over the horizontal stabilizer due to the low speed, the disturbed airflow that results from idling propellers may degrade elevator effectiveness to the extent that you will be unable to flare. That's hard on nosewheels.

Congratulations!

Appendix A
GLOSSARY

Absolute ceiling: The altitude at which the airplane will no longer climb with maximum available power applied.

Accessory case: Usually found at the rear of the engine, this is where the drives for the magnetos, engine-driven pumps, etc., are located.

Accumulator, unfeathering: A system which will drive a feathered propeller toward the unfeathered position without the use of the starter or diving in an attempt to windmill the propeller.

Best angle of climb speed (Vx): That speed which results in the greatest altitude gained per unit of distance.

Best rate of climb speed (Vy): That speed that results in the greatest altitude gained per unit of time.

Blue line airspeed: Best rate of climb with an engine out (Vyse). Marked by a blue radial line on the airspeed indicator.

Coarse pitch: The low-RPM setting of the propeller control. Cruise settings are relatively coarse.

Constant speed propeller: Also called a variable pitch propeller. In order to maintain a constant rotational speed selected by the pilot, blade angle is changed by a governor.

Cowl flaps: Adjustable doors on the bottom of the engine nacelle which admit additional cooling air when needed.

Critical altitude: The altitude at which the turbocharger waste gate is fully closed, providing maximum boost. Above this altitude, engine power will diminish.

Critical engine: The engine which will cause you the most grief if it fails. If both propellers rotate clockwise, the left engine is the critical engine. Airplanes with counter-rotating propellers (or centerline mounted engines) have no critical engine.

Crossfeed: Operating an engine on fuel drawn from a tank on the opposite wing. Usually used to maintain lateral weight distribution when one engine is inoperative. Cannot be used to transfer fuel between tanks.

Drift down: Descent to the absolute ceiling with an engine out.

Empennage: The vertical fin, rudder, horizontal stabilizer, and elevator. The "tail feathers."

Excess horsepower: Power in excess of that necessary to sustain the airplane in level flight.

Flat pitch: That propeller pitch position which results in high RPM; it is the takeoff and short-final setting of the propeller control. Occasionally referred to as "fine pitch."

Flat plate drag: Drag which is developed by the propeller disc when the propeller is driving the engine (or windmilling).

Heavy twin: A multiengine airplane that weighs between 6,000 and 12,500 pounds for takeoff.

Induced drag: The price we pay for lift. Induced drag varies directly with angle of attack, and accordingly is greatest at low speeds and least at cruise speeds.

Intercooler: A heat exchanger. Air heated in the turbocharger's compressor stage passes through the intercooler on its way to the intake manifold, and is cooled as outside air is directed over the intercooler's surface.

ISA: International Standard Atmosphere. The standard pressure and temperature used to determine performance. You are most familiar with its application at sea level (29.92 and 59 degrees Fahrenheit, remember?)

Light twin: A multiengine airplane with a maximum gross takeoff weight of less than 6,000 pounds or which stalls at less than 61 knots. Not to be confused with the distinction between a small airplane and a large airplane, in which the break-point is 12,500 pounds.

A Duchess is a light twin; a Navajo is a heavy twin.

Manifold pressure: The absolute pressure in the induction system of a piston engine. In a normally-aspirated engine, manifold pressure at full throttle will be almost equal to the pressure outside the airplane, making it (at one inch of manifold pressure equals 1000 feet of altitude) a rudimentary altimeter in an emergency.

Minimum controllable airspeed (Vmc): Lowest speed at which the airplane is controllable with one engine developing takeoff power and the other engine's propeller is windmilling. Marked by a red radial line on the airspeed indicator.

Normally aspirated: An engine that breathes by sucking in air. The descending piston does the same thing for the cylinder that your diaphragm does for your lungs.

P-Factor: The force exerted by the downward-moving propeller blade. It increases as the angle of attack of the propeller blade increases.

Parasite drag: Drag caused by skin friction and the aircraft structure itself. Engine cooling air accounts for the largest percentage of parasite drag. Because total parasite drag is a function of airspeed, it is least at low speeds and greatest at high speeds.

Power loading: Gross weight divided by total engine horsepower.

Propeller disc: The invisible disc formed by a rotating propeller (keep all parts of your body outside of the propeller disc). Visualizing the propeller disc helps understand the effects of airflow over that portion of the wing behind the disc and on the empennage.

Service ceiling: The altitude at which the climb rate has diminished to 50 feet per minute.

Waste gate: A means of diverting a variable amount of exhaust gasses over the turbocharger's turbine. When it is open, all gasses go directly to the atmosphere; when it is closed, the maximum designed quantity of exhaust gasses pass over the turbine wheel.

Yaw: Left-right rotation of the airplane around the vertical axis. Seen from the cockpit as left-right motion of the nose of the airplane.

Zero fuel weight: The maximum weight of the airplane before any fuel is loaded into the wing tanks. If your airplane has a fuselage tank, its contents are included in the zero fuel weight.

Zero thrust: An experimentally-derived power setting which simulates operations with one propeller feathered, while keeping the engine ready for use.

Appendix B

AIRPLANE MULTIENGINE LAND (AMEL)

PRACTICAL TEST STANDARD

NOTE: An applicant seeking initial certification as a private pilot in a multiengine land airplane will be evaluated in all TASKS within this standard.

An applicant seeking the addition of a multiengine class rating will not be evaluated on those AREAS OF OPERATIONS/TASKS so noted.

FOREWORD

This Private Pilot Practical Test Standards book has been published by the Federal Aviation Administration (FAA) to establish the standards for the private pilot certification practical tests for all aircraft categories and classes. FAA inspectors and designated pilot examiners will conduct practical tests in compliance with these standards. Flight instructors and applicants will find these standards helpful in practical test preparation.

William T. Brennan
Acting Director, Officer of Flight Standards

INTRODUCTION

The Aviation Standards National Field Office of the FAA has developed this practical test book as a standard to be used by FAA inspectors and designated pilot examiners when conducting airman practical tests (oral and flight tests). Flight instructors are expected to use this book when preparing applicants for practical tests.

This test book contains nine standards that set forth the practical test requirements for private pilot certification in all aircraft categories and associated classes.

For the purpose of private pilot certification practical testing, the following flight test guides were superseded September 1, 1985:

AC 61-54A	Private Pilot — Airplane (4-18-75)
AC 61-59A	Private and Commercial — Helicopter (3-3-77)
AC 61-60	Private and Commercial Pilot — Gyroplane (May 1973)
AC 61-61A	Private and Commercial Pilot — Glider (12-17-76)
AC 61-62A	Private and Commercial Pilot — Free Balloon (12-17-76)
AC 61-63	Private and Commercial Pilot — Lighter-Than-Air Airship (5-23-74)

FAA-S-8081-1A

The FAA gratefully acknowledges the valuable assistance provided by organizations and individuals who have contributed their time and talent in development of the practical test standards.

Comments regarding the Practical Test Standards (AMEL) should be directed to:

U.S. Department of Transportation
Federal Aviation Administration
Aviation Standards National Field Office
Examinations Standards Branch, AVN-130
P.O. Box 25082
Oklahoma City, OK 73125

PRACTICAL TEST STANDARD CONCEPT

FAR's (Federal Aviation Regulations) specify the areas in which knowledge and skill must be demonstrated by the applicant before the issuance of a pilot certificate or rating. The FAR's provide the flexibility to permit the FAA to publish practical test standards containing specific TASKS (procedures and maneuvers) in which pilot competency must be demonstrated. The FAA will add, delete, or revise TASKS whenever it is determined that changes are needed in the interest of safety. Adherence to provisions of the regulations and the practical test standards is mandatory for the evaluation of pilot applicants.

FLIGHT INSTRUCTOR RESPONSIBILITY

An appropriately rated flight instructor is responsible for training the student to the acceptable standards as outlined in the objective of each TASK within the appropriate practical test standard. The flight instructor must certify that the applicant is able to perform safely as a private pilot and is competent to pass the required practical test for the certificate or rating sought.

EXAMINER[1] RESPONSIBILITY

The examiner who conducts the practical test is responsible for determining that the applicant meets standards outlined in the objective of each TASK within the appropriate practical test standard. The examiner shall meet this responsibility by accomplishing an ACTION that is appropriate for each TASK. For each TASK that involves "knowledge only" elements, the examiner will orally quiz the applicant on those elements. For each TASK that involves both "knowledge and skill" elements, the examiner will orally quiz the applicant regarding knowledge elements and ask the applicant to perform the skill elements. The examiner will determine that the applicant's knowledge and skill meets the objective in all required TASKS. Oral questioning may be used at any time during the practical test.

---

[1] *The word "examiner" is used to denote either the FAA inspector or FAA designated pilot examiner who conducts an official flight test.*

INTRODUCTION

PRACTICAL TEST BOOK DESCRIPTION

This test book contains the following private pilot practical test standards:

Section 1   Airplane, Multiengine Land

The looseleaf feature of this test book enables the incorporation of changes which will be sold, as required. This will permit the dissemination of information concerning changes in regulations, pilot certification procedures, and other areas related to safety upon which emphasis should be placed.

PRATICAL TEST STANDARD DESCRIPTION

The AREAS OF OPERATION are phases of flight arranged in a logical sequence within each standard. They begin with the preparation of the flight and end with the conclusion of the flight. The examiner, however, may conduct the practical test in any sequence that results in a complete and efficient test.

The TASKS are procedures and maneuvers appropriate to an AREA OF OPERATION. The AIRCRAFT CATEGORIES AND CLASSES appropriate to the TASKS are abbreviated in capital letters within parentheses immediately following each TASK. The meaning of each abbreviation follows:

ASEL	Airplane Single-Engine Land
AMEL	Airplane Multiengine Land
ASES	Airplane Single-Engine Sea
AMES	Airplane Multiengine Sea
RH	Rotorcraft Helicopter
RG	Rotorcraft Gyroplane
G	Glider (including powered glider)
LA	Lighter-Than-Air Airship
LB	Lighter-Than-Air Free Balloon

The number after the pilot operation relates that TASK to the regulatory requirement.

The REFERENCE identifies the publication(s) that describe(s) the TASK. Descriptions of TASKS are not included in the standards because this information can be found in the listed references. Publications other than those listed may be used for references if their content conveys substantially the same meaning as the referenced publications.

References upon which this practical test book is based include:

FAR Part 61	Certification: Pilots and Flight Instructors
FAR Part 91	General Operating and Flight Rules
AC 00-6	Aviation Weather
AC 00-45	Aviation Weather Services *continued on next page*

AC 61-13	Basic Helicopter Handbook
AC 61-21	Flight Training Handbook
AC 61-23	Pilot's Handbook of Aeronautical Knowledge
AC 61-27	Instrument Flying Handbook
AC 61-84	Role of Preflight Preparation
AC 67-2	Medical Handbook for Pilots
AC 91-13	Cold Weather Operation of Aircraft
AC 91-55	Reduction of Electrical Systems Failure Following Engine Starting
AIM	Airman's Information Manual

NOTE: The latest revision of the references cited should be used.

The OBJECTIVE lists, in sequence, the important elements that must be satisfactorily performed to demonstrate competency in a TASK. The OBJECTIVE includes:

(1) specifically what the applicant should be able to do,
(2) the conditions under which the TASK is to be performed, and
(3) the minimum acceptable standards of performance.

USE OF THE PRACTICAL TEST BOOK

The FAA requires that each practical test be conducted in strict compliance with the appropriate practical test standards for the issuance of a pilot certificate or rating. When using the practical test book, the examiner must evaluate the applicant's knowledge and skill in sufficient depth to determine that the standards of performance listed for all TASKS are met.

When the examiner determines, during the performance of one TASK that the knowledge and skill objective of another TASK is met, it may not be necessary to require the performance of the other TASK.

The examiner may, for any valid reason, elect to evaluate certain TASKS orally, such TASKS include those that do not conform to the manufacturer's recommendations or operating limitations or those that are impracticable, such as night flying, operations over congested areas, or unsuitable terrain, etc.

The examiner is not required to follow the precise order in which the AREAS OF OPERATION and TASKS appear in each section. The examiner may change the sequence or combine TASKS with similar objectives to conserve time. Examiners will develop a plan of action that includes the order and combination of TASKS to be demonstrated by the applicant in a manner that will result in an efficient and valid test. The examiner shall accurately evaluate the applicant's ability to perform safely as a pilot throughout the practical test.

INTRODUCTION

Suggested examples of combining TASKS are:

(1) descending turns may be combined with high altitude emergencies;
(2) rectangular course may be combined with airport traffic pattern; and
(3) navigation during flight by reference to instruments may be combined with visual navigation.

Other TASKS with similar OBJECTIVES may be combined to conserve time. However, the OBJECTIVES of all TASKS must be demonstrated and evaluated at some time during the practical test.

Examiners will place special emphasis upon areas of aircraft operation which are most critical to flight safety. Among these areas are correct aircraft control and sound judgment in decision making. Although these areas may not be shown under each TASK, they are essential to flight safety and will receive careful evaluation throughout the practical test. If these areas are shown in the OBJECTIVE, additional emphasis will be placed on them. THE EXAMINER WILL ALSO EMPHASIZE STALL/ SPIN AWARENESS, SPATIAL DISORIENTATION, COLLISION AVOIDANCE, WAKE TURBULENCE AVOIDANCE, LOW-LEVEL WIND SHEAR, USE OF THE CHECKLIST, AND OTHER AREAS AS DIRECTED BY FUTURE REVISIONS OF THIS STANDARD.

USE OF DISTRACTIONS DURING PRACTICAL TESTS

Numerous studies indicate that many accidents have occurred when the pilot's attention has been distracted during various phases of flight. Many accidents have resulted from engine failure during takeoffs and landings where safe flight was possible if the pilot had used correct control technique and divided attention properly.

Distractions that have been found to cause problems are:

(1) preoccupation with situations inside or outside the cockpit;
(2) maneuvering to avoid other traffic; or
(3) maneuvering to clear obstacles during takeoffs, climbs, approaches, or landings.

To strengthen this area of pilot training and evaluation, the examiner will provide realistic distractions throughout the practical test. Many distractions may he used to evaluate the applicant's ability to divide attention while maintaining safe flight. Some examples of distractions are:

(1) simulating engine failure;
(2) simulating radio tuning and communications;
(3) identifying a field suitable for emergency landings;
(4) identifying features or objects on the ground;
(5) reading the outside air temperature gauge;
(6) removing objects from the glove compartment or map case; and
(7) questioning by the examiner.

PRACTICAL TEST PREREQUISITES

An applicant for a private pilot practical test is required by FAR's to:

(1) pass the appropriate pilot written test since the beginning of the 24th month before the month in which the flight test is taken;
(2) obtain the applicable instruction and aeronautical experience prescribed for the pilot certificate or rating sought;
(3) possess a current medical certificate appropriate to the certificate or rating sought;
(4) meet the age requirement for the issuance of the certificate or rating sought; and
(5) obtain a written statement from an appropriately certificated flight instructor certifying that the applicant has been given flight instruction in preparation for the practical test within 60 days preceding the date of application. The statement shall also state that the instructor finds the applicant competent to pass the practical test, and that the applicant has satisfactory knowledge of the subject area(s) in which a deficiency was indicated by the airman written test report.

NOTE: AC 61-65, Certification: Pilots and Flight Instructors, states that the instructor may sign the instructor's recommendation on the reverse side of FAA Form 8710-1, Airman Certificate and/or Rating Application, in lieu of the previous statement provided, all appropriate FAR Part 61 requirements are substantiated by reliable records.

AIRCRAFT AND EQUIPMENT REQUIREMENTS FOR THE PRACTICAL TEST

The applicant is required to provide an appropriate and airworthy aircraft for the practical test. The aircraft must be equipped for, and its operating limitations must not prohibit the pilot operations required on the test.

SATISFACTORY PERFORMANCE

The ability of an applicant to perform the required TASKS is based on:

(1) executing TASKS within the aircraft's performance capabilities and limitations, including use of the aircraft's systems;
(2) executing emergency procedures and maneuvers appropriate to the aircraft;
(3) piloting the aircraft with smoothness and accuracy;
(4) exercising good judgment;
(5) applying aeronautical knowledge; and
(6) showing mastery of the aircraft within the standards outlined in this book, with the successful outcome of a TASK never seriously in doubt.

INTRODUCTION

UNSATISFACTORY PERFORMANCE

If, in the judgment of the examiner, the applicant does not meet the standards of performance of any TASK performed, the associated PILOT OPERATION is failed and therefore, the practical test is failed.

The examiner or applicant may discontinue the test at any time after the failure of a PILOT OPERATION makes the applicant ineligible for the certificate or rating sought. The test will be continued ONLY with the consent of the applicant. If the test is discontinued, the applicant is entitled to credit for only those TASKS satisfactorily performed. However, during the retest and at the discretion of the examiner, any TASK may be re-evaluated, including those previously passed.

The tolerances stated in the OBJECTIVE represent the minimum performance expected in good flying conditions.

Consistently exceeding tolerances or failure to take prompt corrective action when tolerances are exceeded, is unsatisfactory performance.

Any action, or lack thereof, by the applicant which requires corrective intervention by the examiner to maintain safe flight will be disqualifying. The applicant shall use proper and effective scanning techniques to clear the area before performing maneuvers. Ineffective performance in these areas will be disqualifying.

RECORDING UNSATISFACTORY PERFORMANCE

The term PILOT OPERATION is used in regulations to denote areas (procedures and maneuvers) in which the applicant must demonstrate competency prior to being issued a pilot certificate. This practical test book uses terms AREA OF OPERATION and TASK to denote areas in which competency must be demonstrated. When a disapproval notice is issued, the examiner will record the applicant's unsatisfactory performance in terms of PILOT OPERATIONS appropriate to the practical test conducted.

CONTENTS

I. PREFLIGHT PREPARATION

- A. Certificates And Documents. B-11
- B. Obtaining Weather Information. B-11
- C. Cross-Country Flight Planning B-12

II. MULTIENGINE OPERATION

- A. Airplane Systems B-13
- B. Emergency Procedures B-13
- C. Normal Procedures B-14
- D. Determining Performance And Flight Planning B-15
- E. Use Of Minimum Equipment List B-15
- F. Flight Principles — Engine Inoperative B-15
- G. Aeromedical Factors B-16

III. GROUND OPERATIONS

- A. Visual Inspection B-17
- B. Cockpit Management B-17
- C. Starting Engines B-18
- D. Taxiing B-18
- E. Pretakeoff Check B-19
- F. Postflight Procedures B-19

IV. AIRPORT AND TRAFFIC PATTERN OPERATIONS

- A. Radio Communications And ATC Light Signals B-21
- B. Traffic Pattern Operations B-21
- C. Airport And Runway Marking And Lighting B-22

V. TAKEOFFS AND CLIMBS

- A. Normal And Crosswind Takeoffs And Climbs B-23
- B. Maximum Performance Takeoff And Climb B-24

VI. CROSS-COUNTRY FLYING

- A. Pilotage And Dead Reckoning B-25
- B. Radio Navigation B-26
- C. Diversion B-26
- D. Lost Procedures B-26

VII. FLIGHT BY REFERENCE TO INSTRUMENTS

- A. Straight-And-Level Flight B-27
- B. Straight, Constant Airspeed Climbs B-27

continued on next page

VII. FLIGHT BY REFERENCE TO INSTRUMENTS (continued)

    C. Straight, Constant Airspeed Descents B-28

    D. Turns To Headings B-28

    E. Unusual Flight Attitudes B-29

    F. Radio Aids And Radar Services B-29

VIII. INSTRUMENT FLIGHT

    A. Engine Failure During Straight-And-Level Flight
       And Turns B-31

    B. Instrument Approach — All Engines Operating B-32

    C. Instrument Approach — One Engine Inoperative B-32

IX. FLIGHT AT CRITICALLY SLOW AIRSPEED

    A. Imminent Stalls, Gear Up And Flaps Up B-35

    B. Imminent Stalls, Gear Down And Full Flaps B-36

    C. Maneuvering During Slow Flight B-36

    D. Constant-Altitude Turns B-37

X. FLIGHT MANEUVERING BY REFERENCE TO GROUND OBJECTS

    A. Rectangular Course B-39

    B. S-Turns Across A Road B-40

    C. Turns Around A Point B-40

XI. NIGHT FLIGHT OPERATIONS

    A. Night Flight B-41

XII. EMERGENCY OPERATIONS

    A. System And Equipment Malfunctions B-43

    B. Maneuvering With One Engine Inoperative B-44

    C. Engine Inoperative Loss Of
       Directional Control Demonstration B-45

    D. Demonstrating the Effects Of Various Airspeeds And
       Configurations During Engine Inoperative Performance B-46

    E. Engine Failure En Route B-46

    F. Engine Failure On Takeoff Before Vmc B-47

    G. Engine Failure After Lift-Off B-47

    H. Approach And Landing With An Inoperative Engine B-48

XIII. APPROACHES AND LANDINGS

    A. Normal And Crosswind Approaches And Landings B-49

    B. Go-around B-50

    C. Maximum Performance Approach And Landing B-50

PRACTICAL TEST CHECKLIST B-51

APPLICANT'S PRACTICAL TEST CHECKLIST B-55

I. AREA OF OPERATION: *PREFLIGHT PREPARATION*

A. TASK: CERTIFICATES AND DOCUMENTS

PILOT OPERATION — 1

REFERENCES: FAR Parts 61 and 91; AC 61-21, AC 61-23; Airplane Handbook and Flight Manual.

Objective. To determine that the applicant:

1. Exhibits knowledge by explaining the appropriate —

    (a) pilot certificate, privileges and limitations.
    (b) medical certificate, class and duration.
    (c) personal pilot logbook or flight record.
    (d) FCC station license and operator's permit, as required.

2. Exhibits knowledge by locating and explaining the significance and importance of the —

    (a) airworthiness and registration certificates.
    (b) operating limitations, handbooks, or manuals.
    (c) equipment list.
    (d) weight and balance data.
    (e) maintenance requirements and appropriate records.

B. TASK: OBTAINING WEATHER INFORMATION

NOTE: This TASK is NOT required for the addition of a multiengine land class rating.

PILOT OPERATION — 1

REFERENCES: AC 00-6, AC 00-45, AC 61-21, AC 61-23, AC 61-84.

Objective. To determine that the applicant:

1. Exhibits knowledge of aviation weather information by obtaining, reading, and analyzing —
   (a) weather reports and forecasts.
   (b) weather charts.
   (c) pilot weather reports.
   (d) SIGMET's and AIRMET's.
   (e) Notices to Airmen.
   (f) wind-shear reports.

2. Makes a competent go/no-go decision based on the available information.

C. TASK: CROSS-COUNTRY FLIGHT PLANNING

NOTE: This TASK is NOT required for the addition of a multiengine land class rating.

PILOT OPERATION — 7

REFERENCES: AC 61-21, AC 61-23, AC 61-84.

Objective. To determine that the applicant:

1. Exhibits knowledge by planning, within 30 minutes, a VFR cross-country flight of a duration near the range of the airplane, considering fuel and loading.
2. Selects and uses current and appropriate aeronautical charts.
3. Plots a course for the intended route of flight with fuel stops, if necessary.
4. Selects prominent en route checkpoints.
5. Computes the flight time, headings, and fuel requirements.
6. Selects appropriate radio navigation aids and communication facilities.
7. Identifies airspace, obstructions, and alternate airports.
8. Extracts pertinent information from the Airport/Facility Directory and other flight publications, including NOTAM's.
9. Completes a navigation log.
10. Completes and files a VFR flight plan.

MULTIENGINE OPERATION (AMEL)

II. AREA OF OPERATION:
MULTIENGINE OPERATION

NOTE: Because elements of aeronautical knowledge important for safe multiengine operation may not have been previously demonstrated, all items contained in this area of operation, applicable to the airplane used, will he evaluated through oral testing.

A. TASK: AIRPLANE SYSTEMS

PILOT OPERATION — 1

REFERENCES: AC 61-21; Airplane Handbook and Flight Manual.

Objective. To determine that the applicant exhibits knowledge by explaining the airplane systems and operation, including, as appropriate:

1. Primary flight controls and trim.
2. Wing flaps, leading edge devices, and spoilers.
3. Flight instruments.
4. Landing gear.
5. Engines.
6. Propellers.
7. Fuel system.
8. Hydraulic system.
9. Electrical system.
10. Environmental system.
11. Oil system.
12. Deice and anti-ice systems.
13. Avionics.
14. Vacuum system.

B. TASK: EMERGENCY PROCEDURES

PILOT OPERATION — 1

REFERENCES: AC 61-21; Airplane Handbook and Flight Manual.

NOTE: Demonstration of intentional spins and recovery are not required on the practical test, and are prohibited. However, the examiner will ask the applicant to explain the recommended spin recovery procedure for the particular airplane used. This knowledge is essential for recovery if an unintentional spin occurs. THIS IS A KNOWLEDGE REQUIREMENT ONLY.

Objective. To determine that the applicant exhibits knowledge by explaining the airplane emergency procedures, as appropriate, including:

1. Emergency checklist.
2. Partial power loss.
3. Engine failure —
   (a) before lift-off.
   (b) after lift-off.
   (c) during climb and cruise.
   (d) during approach and landing.
4. Engine securing and restart.
5. Emergency landing —
   (a) precautionary.
   (b) without power.
   (c) ditching.
6. Engine roughness or overheat.
7. Loss of oil pressure.
8. Smoke and fire.
9. Icing.
10. Crossfeed.
11. Pressurization.
12. Emergency descent.
13. Pilot static system and instruments.
14. Electrical.
15. Landing gear.
16. Wing flaps (asymmetrical position).
17. Inadvertent door openings.
18. Emergency equipment and exits.
19. Recommended recovery procedure for an unintentional spin.

C. TASK: NORMAL PROCEDURES

PILOT OPERATION — 1

REFERENCES: AC 61-21; Airplane Handbook and Flight Manual.

Objective. To determine that the applicant exhibits knowledge by explaining the airplane normal operating procedures, including:

1. Airspeeds for safe operations, airspeed symbols and definitions.
2. Operating and airplane limitations, reasons for limitations.
3. Applicable warnings, cautions, or placards.
4. Use of auxiliary power for starting.
5. Taxi procedures and precautions.
6. Takeoff profile.
7. Environmental systems.
8. Noise abatement procedures.

D. TASK: DETERMINING PERFORMANCE AND FLIGHT PLANNING

PILOT OPERATION — 1

REFERENCES: AC 61-21; Airplane Handbook and Flight Manual.

Objective. To determine that the applicant:

1. Calculates airplane performance in all phases of flight, including —

    (a) accelerate-stop distance.
    (b) accelerate-go distance.
    (c) takeoff performance, all engines, single-engine.
    (d) climb performance, all engines, single-engine.
    (e) service ceiling, all engines, single-engine.
    (f) cruise performance.
    (g) fuel consumption, range, endurance.
    (h) descent performance.
    (i) go-around performance.
    (j) landing distance.

2. Computes weight and balance for all phases of flight, including —

    (a) adding, removing, and shifting weight.
    (b) determining that weight and center of gravity are within limits.

E. TASK: USE OF MINIMUM EQUIPMENT LIST

PILOT OPERATION — 1

REFERENCE: FAR Section 91.30.

Objective. To determine that the applicant exhibits knowledge of the elements related to the use of an approved minimum equipment list, including:

1. The airworthiness limitations imposed on multiengine aircraft operations with inoperative instruments or equipment.
2. The district office letter of authorization requirement.
3. Supplemental type certificate.
4. Instrument and equipment exemptions.
5. Special flight permit.

F. TASK: FLIGHT PRINCIPLES — ENGINE INOPERATIVE

PILOT OPERATION — 1

REFERENCES: AC 61-21; Airplane Handbook and Flight Manual.

Objective. To determine that the applicant exhibits knowledge by explaining the flight principles related to operation with an engine inoperative, including:

1. Factors affecting single-engine flight —
    (a) density altitude.
    (b) drag reduction.

Factors affecting single-engine flight *(continued)*

    (c) airspeed (Vsse, Vxse, Vyse, Vmc).
    (d) aircraft control.
    (e) weight and center of gravity.
    (f) critical engine.

2. Directional control —
    (a) reasons for loss of directional control.
    (b) reasons for variations in Vmc.
    (c) indications of approaching loss of directional control.
    (d) safe recovery procedure, if directional control is lost.
    (e) Vmc in relation to stall speed.
    (f) whether an engine inoperative loss of directional control demonstration can be safely accomplished in flight.

3. Takeoff emergencies —
    (a) takeoff planning.
    (b) decisions after engine failure.
    (c) single-engine operation.

G. TASK: AEROMEDICAL FACTORS

NOTE: This TASK is not required for the addition of a multiengine land class rating.

PILOT OPERATION — 1

REFERENCES: AC 61-21, AC 67-2; AIM.

Objective. To determine that the applicant:

1. Exhibits knowledge of the elements related to aeromedical factors, including the symptoms, effects, and corrective action of —
    (a) hypoxia.
    (b) hyperventilation.
    (c) middle ear and sinus problems.
    (d) spatial disorientation.
    (e) motion sickness.
    (f) carbon monoxide poisoning.

2. Exhibits knowledge of the effects of alcohol and drugs, and the relationship to flight safety.

3. Exhibits knowledge of nitrogen excesses during scuba dives, and how this affects a pilot or passenger during flight.

GROUND OPERATIONS (AMEL)

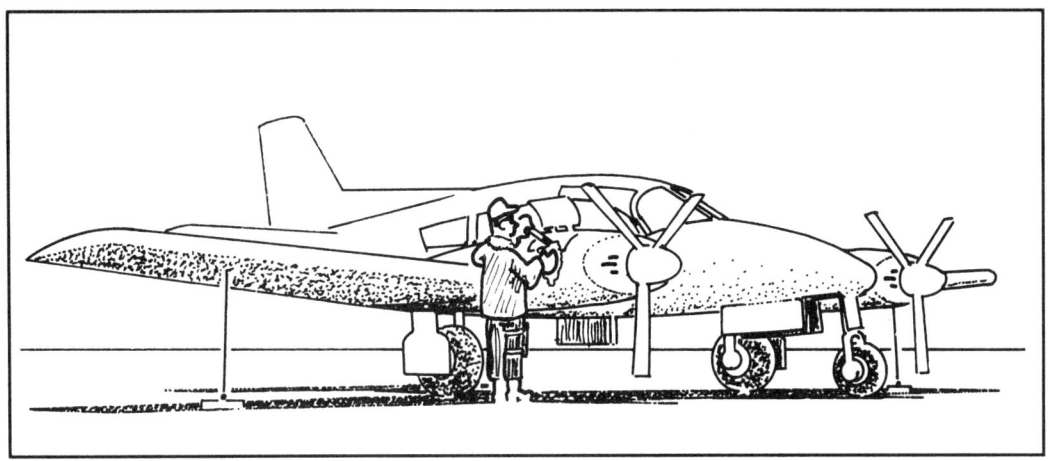

III. AREA OF OPERATION: *GROUND OPERATIONS*

A. TASK: VISUAL INSPECTION

PILOT OPERATION — 1

REFERENCES: AC 61-21; Airplane Handbook and Flight Manual.

Objective. To determine that the applicant:

1. Exhibits knowledge of airplane visual inspection by explaining the reasons for checking all items.
2. Inspects the airplane by following a checklist.
3. Determines that the airplane is in condition for safe flight, emphasizing —

   (a) fuel quantity, grade, and type.
   (b) fuel contamination safeguards.
   (c) oil quantity, grade, and type.
   (d) fuel, oil, and hydraulic leaks.
   (e) flight controls.
   (f) structural damage.
   (g) tiedown, control lock, and wheel chock removal.
   (h) ice and frost removal.
   (i) security of baggage, cargo, and equipment.

B. TASK: COCKPIT MANAGEMENT

PILOT OPERATION — 1

REFERENCE: AC 61-21.

Objective. To determine that the applicant:

1. Exhibits knowledge of cockpit management by explaining related safety and efficiency factors.
2. Organizes and arranges the material and equipment in an efficient manner.
3. Ensures that the safety belts and shoulder harnesses are fastened.

THE COMPLETE MULTIENGINE PILOT

B. TASK: COCKPIT MANAGEMENT *(continued)*

4. Adjusts and locks rudder pedals and pilot's seat to a safe position and ensures full control movement.
5. Briefs occupants on the use of safety belts and emergency procedures.
6. Exhibits adequate crew coordination.

C. TASK: STARTING ENGINES

PILOT OPERATION — 1

REFERENCES: AC 61-21, AC 91-13, AC 91-55; Airplane Handbook and Flight Manual.

Objective. To determine that the applicant:

1. Exhibits knowledge by explaining engine starting procedures, including starting under various atmospheric conditions.
2. Performs all the items on the checklist.
3. Accomplishes correct starting procedures with emphasis on —
    (a) positioning the airplane to avoid creating hazards.
    (b) determining that the area is clear.
    (c) adjusting the engine controls.
    (d) setting the brakes.
    (e) preventing airplane movement after engine start.
    (f) avoiding excessive engine RPM and temperatures.
    (g) checking engine instruments after engine start.

D. TASK: TAXIING

PILOT OPERATION — 2

REFERENCE: AC 61-21.

Objective. To determine that the applicant:

1. Exhibits knowledge by explaining safe taxi procedures.
2. Adheres to signals and clearances and follows the proper taxi route.
3. Performs brake check after the airplane begins moving.
4. Controls taxi speed without excessive use of brakes.
5. Recognizes and avoids hazards.
6. Positions controls for existing wind conditions.
7. Uses differential power, when necessary.
8. Checks instruments for proper operation.
9. Avoids careless and reckless operations.

GROUND OPERATIONS (AMEL)

E. TASK: PRETAKEOFF CHECK

PILOT OPERATION — 1

REFERENCES: AC 61-21; Airplane Handbook and Flight Manual.

Objective. To determine that the applicant:

1. Exhibits knowledge of the pretakeoff check by explaining the reasons for checking all items.
2. Positions airplane to avoid creating hazards.
3. Divides attention inside and outside of the cockpit.
4. Accomplishes the checklist items.
5. Ensures that the airplane is in safe operating condition.
6. Reviews the critical takeoff performance airspeeds, takeoff distances, and emergency procedures.
7. Ensures takeoff path is free of hazards.
8. Obtains and interprets takeoff and departure clearance.

F. TASK: POSTFLIGHT PROCEDURES

PILOT OPERATION — 3

REFERENCES: AC 61-21; Airplane Handbook and Flight Manual.

Objective. To determine that the applicant:

1. Exhibits knowledge by explaining the postflight procedures, including taxiing, parking, shutdown, securing, and postflight inspection.
2. Selects and taxies to the designated or suitable parking area, considering wind conditions and obstructions.
3. Parks the airplane properly.
4. Follows the recommended procedure for engine shutdown, cockpit securing, and deplaning passengers.
5. Secures the airplane properly.
6. Performs a satisfactory postflight inspection.

AIRPOIRT AND TRAFFIC PATTERN OPERATIONS (AMEL)

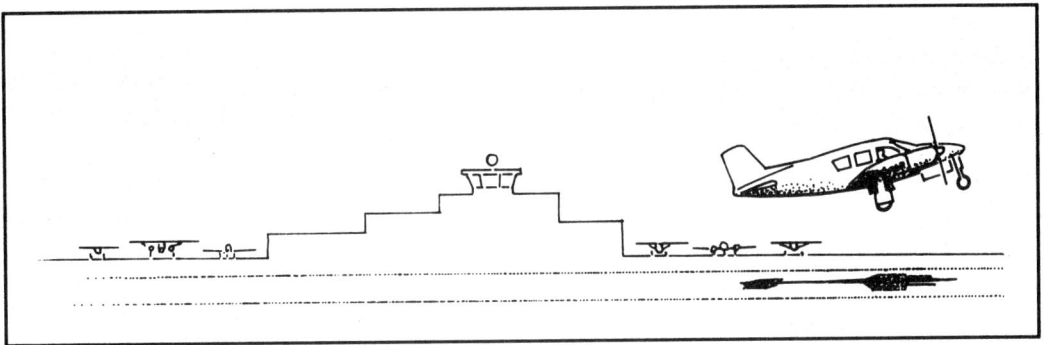

IV. AREA OF OPERATION:
AIRPORT AND TRAFFIC PATTERN OPERATIONS

NOTE: This AREA OF OPERATION is NOT required for the addition of a multiengine land class rating.

A. TASK: RADIO COMMUNICATIONS AND ATC LIGHT SIGNALS

PILOT OPERATION — 2

REFERENCES: AC 61-21, AC 61-23; AIM.

Objective. To determine that the applicant:

1. Exhibits knowledge by explaining radio communication, ATC light signals, procedures at controlled and uncontrolled airports, and prescribed procedures for radio failure.
2. Selects the appropriate frequencies for the facilities to be used.
3. Transmits requests and reports using the recommended standard phraseology.
4. Receives, acknowledges, and complies with radio communications.

B. TASK: TRAFFIC PATTERN OPERATIONS

PILOT OPERATION — 2

REFERENCES: AC 61-21, AC 61-23; AIM.

Objective. To determine that the applicant:

1. Exhibits knowledge by explaining traffic pattern procedures at controlled and uncontrolled airports, including collision, wake turbulence, and windshear avoidance.
2. Follows the established traffic pattern procedures according to instructions or rules.
3. Corrects for wind drift to follow the appropriate ground track.
4. Maintains proper spacing from other traffic.
5. Maintains the traffic pattern altitude, ± 100 feet.
6. Maintains the desired airspeed, ± 10 knots.
7. Completes the prelanding checklist.
8. Maintains orientation with the runway in use.

C. TASK: AIRPORT AND RUNWAY MARKING AND LIGHTING

PILOT OPERATION — 2

REFERENCES: AC 61-21; AIM.

Objective. To determine that the applicant:

1. Exhibits knowledge by explaining airport and runway markings and lighting aids.
2. Identifies and interprets airport, runway, taxiway marking and lighting aids.

TAKEOFFS AND CLIMBS (AMEL)

V. AREA OF OPERATION: *TAKEOFFS AND CLIMBS*

A. TASK: NORMAL AND CROSSWIND TAKEOFFS AND CLIMBS

PILOT OPERATION — 5

REFERENCE: AC 61-21.

Objective. To determine that the applicant:

1. Exhibits knowledge by explaining the elements of normal and crosswind takeoffs and climbs, including airspeeds, configurations, and emergency procedures.
2. Aligns the airplane on the runway centerline.
3. Applies full aileron deflection in proper direction.
4. Advances the throttles smoothly to maximum allowable power.
5. Checks engine instruments.
6. Maintains directional control on the runway centerline.
7. Adjusts aileron deflection during acceleration.
8. Rotates at the airspeed to attain lift-off at Vmc, +5 or the recommended[1] lift-off airspeed.
9. Accelerates to Vy, ± 5 knots.
10. Retracts the wing flaps, as recommended, and at a safe altitude.
11. Retracts the landing gear after a positive rate of climb has been established and a safe landing cannot be made on the remaining runway, or as recommended.
12. Climbs at Vy, ± 5 knots, to a safe maneuvering altitude.
13. Maintains takeoff power to a safe maneuvering altitude.
14. Uses noise abatement procedures, as required.
15. Establishes and maintains a recommended climb airspeed, ± 5 knots.
16. Maintains a straight track over the extended runway centerline until a turn is required.
17. Completes after-takeoff checklist.

NOTE: If a crosswind condition does not exist, the applicant's knowledge of the TASK will be evaluated through oral testing.

---

[1] The term "recommended" refers to the manufacturer's recommendation. If the manufacturer's recommendation is not available, the description contained in AC 61-21 will be used.

B. TASK: MAXIMUM PERFORMANCE TAKEOFF AND CLIMB

PILOT OPERATION — 8

REFERENCE: AC 61-21.

Objective. To determine that the applicant:

1. Exhibits knowledge by explaining the elements of a maximum performance takeoff and climb, including airspeeds, configurations, and expected performance for specified operating conditions.
2. Positions the airplane at the beginning of the takeoff runway aligned on the runway centerline.
3. Advances the throttles smoothly to maximum allowable power.
4. Checks engine instruments.
5. Maintains directional control on the runway centerline.
6. Rotates at the airspeed to attain lift-off at Vmc +5 knots, Vx or at the recommended airspeed.
7. Climbs at Vx + 5, - 0 knots, or the recommended airspeed, whichever is greater until specified obstacle is cleared, then accelerates to Vy, ± 5 knots.
8. Retracts the wing flaps, as recommended, and at a safe altitude.
9. Retracts the landing gear after a positive rate of climb has been established and a safe landing cannot be made on the remaining runway, or as recommended.
10. Climbs at Vy, ± 5 knots, to a safe maneuvering altitude.
11. Maintains takeoff power to a safe maneuvering altitude.
12. Uses noise abatement procedures, as required.
13. Establishes and maintains a recommended climb airspeed, ± 5 knots.
14. Maintains a straight track over the extended runway centerline until a turn is required.
15. Completes after-takeoff checklist.

VI. AREA OF OPERATION: *CROSS-COUNTRY FLYING*

NOTE: This AREA OF OPERATION is NOT required for the addition of a multiengine land class rating.

A. TASK: PILOTAGE AND DEAD RECKONING

PILOT OPERATION — 7

REFERENCES: AC 61-21, AC 61-23.

Objective. To determine that the applicant:

1. Exhibits knowledge by explaining pilotage and dead reckoning techniques and procedures.
2. Follows the preplanned course solely by visual reference to landmarks.
3. Identifies landmarks by relating the surface features to chart symbols.
4. Navigates by means of precomputed headings, groundspeed, and elapsed time.
5. Combines pilotage and dead reckoning.
6. Verifies the airplane position within 3 nautical miles of the flight planned route at all times.
7. Arrives at the en route checkpoints and destination, ± 5 minutes of the initial or revised ETA.
8. Corrects for, and records, the differences between preflight fuel, groundspeed, and heading calculations and those determined en route.
9. Maintains the selected altitudes, within ± 200 feet.
10. Maintains the desired heading, ± 10 degrees.
11. Follows the climb, cruise, and descent checklists.

B. TASK: RADIO NAVIGATION

PILOT OPERATION — 7

REFERENCES: AC 61-21, AC 61-23.

Objective. To determine that the applicant:

1. Exhibits knowledge by explaining radio navigation, equipment, procedures, and limitations.
2. Selects and identifies the desired radio facility.
3. Locates position relative to the radio navigation facility.
4. Intercepts and tracks a given radial or bearing.
5. Locates position using cross radials or bearings.
6. Recognizes or describes the indication of station passage.
7. Recognizes signal loss and takes appropriate action.
8. Maintains the appropriate altitude ± 200 feet.

C. TASK: DIVERSION

PILOT OPERATION — 7

REFERENCES: AC 61-21, AC 61-23.

Objective. To determine that the applicant:

1. Exhibits knowledge by explaining the procedures for diverting, including the recognition of adverse weather conditions.
2. Selects an appropriate alternate airport and route.
3. Diverts toward the alternate airport promptly.
4. Makes a reasonable estimate of heading, groundspeed, arrival time, and fuel consumption to the alternate airport.
5. Maintains the appropriate altitude ± 200 feet.

D. TASK: LOST PROCEDURES

PILOT OPERATION — 7

REFERENCES: AC 61-21, AC 61-23.

Objective. To determine that the applicant:

1. Exhibits knowledge by explaining lost procedures, including the reason for —
   (a) maintaining the original or an appropriate heading, identifying land marks, and climbing, if necessary.
   (b) proceeding to and identifying the nearest concentration of prominent landmarks.
   (c) using available radio navigation aids or contacting an appropriate facility for assistance.
   (d) planning a precautionary landing if deteriorating visibility and/or fuel exhaustion is imminent.
2. Selects the best course of action when given a lost situation.

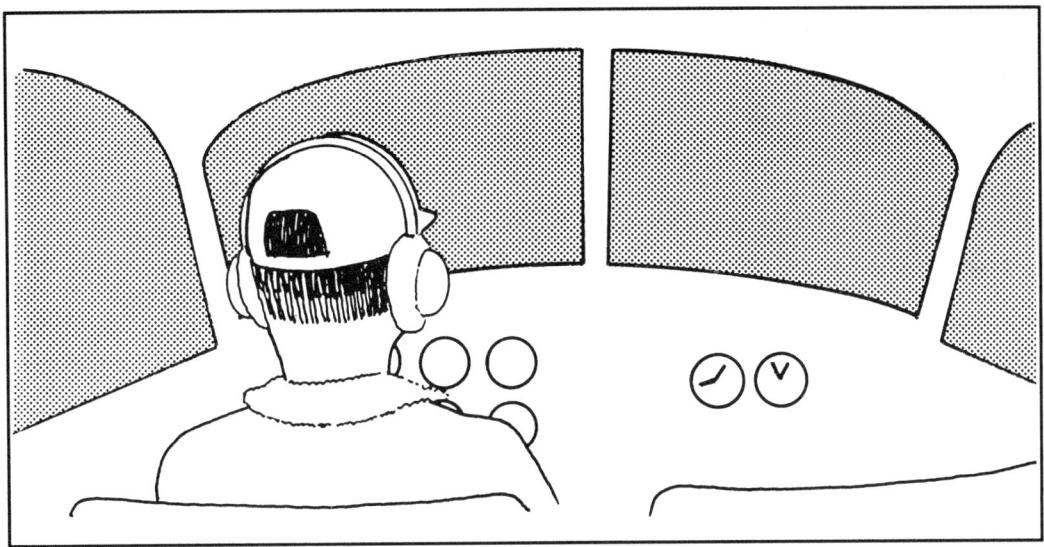

VII. AREA OF OPERATION: *FLIGHT BY REFERENCE TO INSTRUMENTS*

NOTE: This AREA OF OPERATION is NOT required for the addition of a multiengine land class rating. It IS required for INITIAL certification as a private pilot in a multiengine land airplane.

A. TASK: STRAIGHT-AND-LEVEL FLIGHT

PILOT OPERATION — 6

REFERENCES: AC 61-21, AC 61-23, AC 61-27.

Objective. To determine that the applicant:

1. Exhibits knowledge by explaining flight solely by reference to instruments as related to straight-and-level flight.
2. Makes smooth and coordinated control applications.
3. Maintains straight-and-level flight for at least 3 minutes.
4. Maintains the desired heading, ± 10 degrees.
5. Maintains the desired altitude, ± 100 feet.
6. Maintains the desired airspeed, ± 10 knots.

B. TASK: STRAIGHT, CONSTANT AIRSPEED CLIMBS

PILOT OPERATION — 6

REFERENCES: AC 61-21, AC 61-23, AC 61-27.

Objective. To determine that the applicant:

1. Exhibits knowledge by explaining flight solely by reference to instruments as related to straight, constant airspeed climbs.
2. Establishes the climb pitch attitude and power setting on an assigned heading.
3. Makes smooth and coordinated control applications.
4. Maintains the desired heading, ± 10 degrees.

B. TASK: STRAIGHT, CONSTANT AIRSPEED CLIMBS (*continued*)

5. Maintains the desired airspeed, ± 10 knots.
6. Levels off at the desired altitude, ± 100 feet.

C. TASK: STRAIGHT, CONSTANT AIRSPEED DESCENTS

PILOT OPERATION — 6

REFERENCES: AC 61-21, AC 61-23, AC 61-27.

Objective. To determine that the applicant:

1. Exhibits knowledge by explaining flight solely by reference to instruments as related to straight, constant airspeed descents.
2. Determines the minimum safe altitude at which the descent should be terminated.
3. Establishes the descent configuration, pitch, and power setting on the assigned heading.
4. Makes smooth and coordinated control application.
5. Maintains the desired heading, ± 10 degrees.
6. Maintains the desired airspeed, ± 10 knots.
7. Levels off at the desired altitude, ± 100 feet.

D. TASK: TURNS TO HEADINGS

PILOT OPERATION — 6

REFERENCES: AC 61-21, AC 61-23, AC 61-27.

Objective. To determine that the applicant:

1. Exhibits knowledge by explaining flight solely by reference to instruments as related to turns to headings.
2. Enters and maintains approximately a standard-rate turn with smooth and coordinated control applications.
3. Maintains the desired altitude, ± 100 feet.
4. Maintains the desired airspeed, ± 10 knots.
5. Maintains the desired bank angle.
6. Rolls out at the desired heading, ± 10 degrees.

FLIGHT BY REFERENCE TO INSTRUMENTS (AMEL)

E. TASK: UNUSUAL FLIGHT ATTITUDES

PILOT OPERATION — 6

REFERENCES: AC 61-21, AC 61-23, AC 61-27.

NOTE: Unusual flight attitudes, such as a start of a power-on spiral or an approach to a climbing stall, shall not exceed 45 degree bank or 10 degree pitch from level flight.

Objective. To determine that the applicant:

1. Exhibits knowledge by explaining flight solely by reference to instruments as related to unusual flight attitudes.
2. Recognizes unusual flight attitudes promptly.
3. Properly interprets the instruments.
4. Recovers to a stabilized level flight attitude by prompt, smooth, coordinated control, applied in the proper sequence.
5. Avoids excessive load factor, airspeed, and stall.

F. TASK: RADIO AIDS AND RADAR SERVICES

PILOT OPERATION — 6

REFERENCES: AC 61-21, AC 61-23, AC 61-27.

Objective. To determine that the applicant:

1. Exhibits knowledge by explaining radio aids and radar services available for use during flight solely by reference to instruments.
2. Selects, tunes, and identifies the appropriate facility.
3. Follows verbal instruction or radio navigation aids for guidance.
4. Determines the minimum safe altitude.
5. Maintains the desired altitude, ± 100 feet.
6. Maintains the desired heading, ± 10 degrees.

INSTRUMENT FLIGHT (AMEL)

VIII. AREA OF OPERATION: *INSTRUMENT FLIGHT*

NOTE: If an applicant holds a private pilot certificate with an airplane single-engine land and instrument rating and seeks to add an airplane multiengine land rating, the applicant is required to demonstrate competency in all TASKS of AREA OF OPERATION VIII.

If the applicant elects not to demonstrate competency in instrument flight, the applicant's multiengine privileges will be limited to VFR only. To remove this restriction, the pilot must demonstrate competency in this AREA OF OPERATION.

If the applicant elects to demonstrate competency in the TASKS of AREA OF OPERATION VIII, then fails one or more of those TASKS, the applicant will have failed the practical test. After the test is initiated, the applicant will not he permitted to revert to the "VFR only" option.

A. TASK: ENGINE FAILURE DURING STRAIGHT-AND-LEVEL FLIGHT AND TURNS

PILOT OPERATION — 10

REFERENCES: FAR Part 61; AC 61-21, AC 61-27.

Objective. To determine that the applicant:

1. Exhibits knowledge of the procedures used if engine failure occurs during straight-and-level flight and turns while on instruments.
2. Recognizes engine failure simulated by the examiner during straight-and-level flight and turns.
3. Sets all engine controls, reduces drag, and identifies and verifies the inoperative engine.
4. Establishes the best engine-inoperative airspeed, and trims the aircraft.
5. Verifies the accomplishment of prescribed checklist procedures for securing the inoperative engine.

ENGINE FAILURE DURING STRAIGHT-AND-LEVEL FLIGHT AND TURN (*continued*)

6. Establishes and maintains the recommended flight attitude, as necessary, for best performance during straight-and-level and turning flight.
7. Attempts to determine the reason for the engine failure.
8. Monitors all engine control functions and makes necessary adjustments.
9. Maintains the specified altitude within ± 100 feet, if within the aircraft capability, airspeed within ± 10 knots, and the desired heading within ± 10 degrees.
10. Assesses the aircraft performance capability, and decides an appropriate action to ensure a safe landing.
11. Avoids imminent loss of aircraft control, or attempted flight contrary to the engine-inoperative operating limitations of the aircraft.

B. TASK: INSTRUMENT APPROACH — ALL ENGINES OPERATING

PILOT OPERATION — 6

REFERENCES: FAR Part 61; AC 61-21, AC 61-27.

Objective. To determine that the applicant:

1. Exhibits knowledge of cockpit management used on an instrument approach in a multiengine airplane.
2. Requests and receives an actual or a simulated ATC clearance for an instrument approach.
3. Follows the actual or simulated ATC clearances and advisories and the published instrument approach procedure.
4. Establishes a rate of descent that will ensure arrival at the MDA or DH with the airplane continuously in a position from which descent to a landing on the intended runway can be made straight-in or circling.
5. Maintains the specified airspeed within ± 10 knots and altitude within ± 100 feet, prior to the final approach fix.
6. Allows less than full-scale deflection of the CDI and the glide slope indicator, or ± 10 degrees of the NDB final approach course.
7. Avoids descent below the published minimum altitude or exceeding the visibility criteria for the aircraft approach category when circling.
8. Executes a missed approach procedure at the designated missed approach point, and follows the appropriate airplane checklist procedures.
9. Sets the navigation and communication equipment used during the approach, and uses the proper communications technique.

C. TASK: INSTRUMENT APPROACH — ONE ENGINE INOPERATIVE

PILOT OPERATION — 10

REFERENCES: FAR Part 61; AC 61-21, AC 61-27.

Objective. To determine that the applicant:

1. Exhibits knowledge by explaining the procedures used during an instrument approach in a multiengine airplane with one engine inoperative.
2. Recognizes promptly engine failure simulated by the examiner.

INSTRUMENT FLIGHT

3. Sets all engine controls, reduces drag, and identifies and verifies the inoperative engine.

4. Establishes the best engine-inoperative airspeed and trims the airplane.

5. Verifies the accomplishment of prescribed checklist procedures for securing the inoperative engine.

6. Establishes and maintains the recommended flight attitude and configuration for the best performance for all maneuvering necessary for the instrument approach procedures.

7. Attempts to determine the reason for the engine failure.

8. Monitors all engine control functions and makes necessary adjustments.

9. Requests, and receives, an actual or a simulated ATC clearance for an instrument approach.

10. Follows the actual or a simulated ATC clearance for an instrument approach.

11. Establishes a rate of descent that will ensure arrival at the MDA or DH with the aircraft continuously in a position from which descent to a landing on the intended runway can be made straight-in or circling.

12. Maintains, where applicable, the specified altitude within ± 100 feet (if within the airplane's capability), the airspeed within ± 10 knots, and heading within ± 10 degrees.

13. Avoids imminent loss of airplane control, or attempted flight contrary to the engine-inoperative operating limitations of the airplane.

14. Complies with the published criteria for the aircraft approach category when circling.

15. Allows less than full-scale deflection of the CDI and the glide slope indicator, or ± 10 degrees of the NDB final approach course.

16. Sets the navigation and communication equipment used during the approach and uses the proper communications technique.

17. Completes a safe landing.

FLIGHT AT CRITICALLY SLOW AIRSPEED

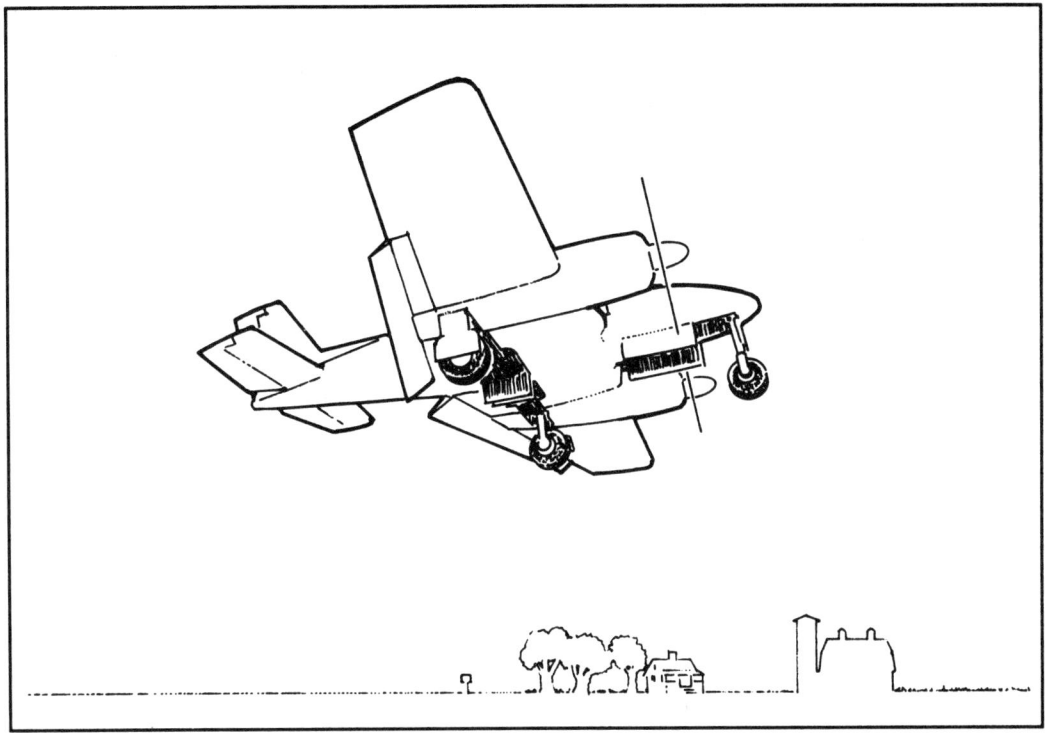

IX. AREA OF OPERATION:
FLIGHT AT CRITICALLY SLOW AIRSPEED

NOTE: No stall will be performed with one engine throttled or inoperative and the other engine(s) developing effective power.

Full stalls using high-power settings have been deleted from the multiengine practical test because of excessive high pitch angles necessary to induce these stalls which may result in uncontrollable flight.

Examiners and instructors should be alert to the possible development of high sink rates during these TASKS.

A. TASK: IMMINENT STALLS, GEAR UP AND FLAPS UP

PILOT OPERATION — 4

REFERENCE: AC 61-21.

Objective. To determine that the applicant:

1. Exhibits knowledge by explaining the aerodynamic factors associated with imminent stalls, gear up and flaps up.
2. Selects an entry altitude that will allow recoveries to be completed no lower than 3,000 feet AGL.
3. Stabilizes approach airspeed in level flight with a gear-up, flaps-up configuration and appropriate power setting.

THE COMPLETE MULTIENGINE PILOT

IMMINENT STALLS, GEAR UP AND FLAPS UP (*continued*)

4. Establishes a pitch attitude, straight ahead or in a turn with a bank angle of 20 degrees, ± 10 degrees that will induce an imminent stall.
5. Maintains desired altitude, ± 100 feet.
6. Applies proper control to maintain coordinated flight.
7. Recognizes and recovers from imminent stalls at the first indication of buffeting or decay of control effectiveness by immediately reducing angle of attack, increasing power, and leveling wings.
8. Returns to entry airspeed, altitude, and configuration.
9. Avoids full stalls, excessive pitch change, excessive altitude loss, spirals, spins, and flight below 3,000 feet AGL.

B. TASK: IMMINENT STALLS, GEAR DOWN AND FULL FLAPS

PILOT OPERATION — 4

REFERENCE: AC 61-21.

Objective. To determine that the applicant:

1. Exhibits knowledge by explaining the aerodynamic factors associated with imminent stalls, gear down and full flaps.
2. Selects an entry altitude that will allow recoveries to be completed no lower than 3,000 feet AGL.
3. Stabilizes the approach airspeed in level flight with a gear down and full flaps configuration and appropriate power setting.
4. Establishes a pitch attitude straight ahead, and in 20 degree bank turns, ± 10 degrees, that will induce a stall.
5. Maintains altitude, ± 100 feet.
6. Applies proper control to maintain coordinated flight.
7. Recognizes and recovers from imminent stalls at the first indication of buffeting or decay of control effectiveness by immediately reducing angle of attack, increasing power, and leveling wings.
8. Returns to entry airspeed, altitude, and configuration.
9. Avoids full stalls, excessive pitch change, excessive altitude loss, spirals, spins, and flight below 3,000 feet AGL.

C. TASK: MANEUVERING DURING SLOW FLIGHT

PILOT OPERATION— 4

REFERENCE: AC 61-21.

Objective. To determine that the applicant:

1. Exhibits knowledge by explaining the flight characteristics and controllability associated with maneuvering during slow flight.
2. Selects an entry altitude that will allow the maneuver to be performed no lower than 3,000 feet AGL.
3. Establishes and maintains slow flight, specified gear position, various flap settings and angle of bank, during straight-and-level flight and level turns.

FLIGHT AT CRITICALLY SLOW AIRSPEED

4. Maintains the specified altitude, ± 100 feet.
5. Maintains the specified heading during straight flight, ± 10 degrees.
6. Maintains the specified bank angle, ± 10 degrees, during turning flight.
7. Maintains an airspeed of 10 knots, ± 5 knots, above stall speed or Vmc, whichever is greater.

D. TASK: CONSTANT-ALTITUDE TURNS

PILOT OPERATION — 2

REFERENCE: AC 61-21.

Objective. To determine that the applicant:

1. Exhibits knowledge by explaining the performance factors associated with constant-altitude turns, including increased load factors, power required and overbanking tendency.
2. Selects an altitude that will allow the maneuver to be performed no lower than 3,000 feet AGL.
3. Establishes an airspeed which does not exceed the airplane design maneuvering airspeed.
4. Enters a 360-degree turn maintaining a bank angle of 40 to 50 degrees in coordinated flight.
5. Divides attention between airplane control and orientation.
6. Rolls out ± 10 degrees of the desired heading.
7. Maintains the desired altitude, ± 100 feet, and airspeed, ± 10 knots.

FLIGHT MANEUVERING BY REFERENCE TO GROUND OBJECTS (AMEL)

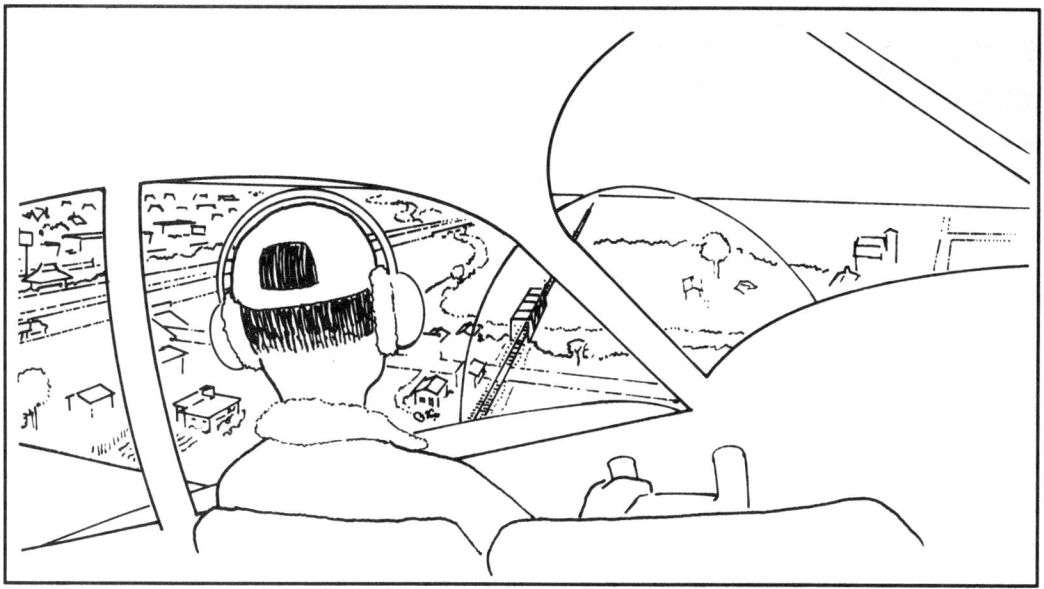

X. AREA OF OPERATION: *FLIGHT MANEUVERING BY REFERENCE TO GROUND OBJECTS*

NOTE: This AREA OF OPERATION is NOT required for the addition of a multiengine land class rating.

A. TASK: RECTANGULAR COURSE

PILOT OPERATION — 3

REFERENCE: AC 61-21.

Objective. To determine that the applicant:

1. Exhibits knowledge by explaining wind-drift correction in straight-and-turning flight and the relationship of the rectangular course to airport traffic patterns.
2. Selects a suitable reference area.
3. Enters a left or right pattern at a desired distance from the selected reference area and at 600 to 1,000 feet AGL.
4. Divides attention between airplane control and ground track, and maintains coordinated flight.
5. Applies the necessary wind-drift corrections during straight-and-turning flight to maintain the desired ground track.
6. Maintains the desired altitude, ± 100 feet.
7. Maintains the desired airspeed, ± 10 knots.
8. Avoids bank angles in excess of 45 degrees.
9. Reverses course, as directed by the examiner.

THE COMPLETE MULTIENGINE PILOT

B. TASK: S-TURNS ACROSS A ROAD

PILOT OPERATION — 3

REFERENCE: AC 61-21.

Objective. To determine that the applicant:

1. Exhibits knowledge by explaining the procedures and wind-drift correction associated with S-turns.
2. Selects a suitable ground reference line.
3. Enters perpendicular to the selected reference line at 600 to 1,000 feet AGL.
4. Divides attention between airplane control and ground track, and maintains coordinated flight.
5. Applies the necessary wind-drift correction to track a constant radius turn on each side of the selected reference line.
6. Reverses the direction of turn directly over the selected reference line.
7. Maintains the desired altitude, ± 100 feet.
8. Maintains the desired airspeed, ± 10 knots.

C. TASK: TURNS AROUND A POINT

PILOT OPERATION — 3

REFERENCE: AC 61-21.

Objective. To determine that the applicant:

1. Exhibits knowledge by explaining the procedures and wind-drift correction associated with turns around a point.
2. Selects a suitable ground reference point.
3. Enters a left or right turn at a desired distance from the selected reference point at 600 to 1,000 feet AGL.
4. Divides attention between airplane control and ground track, and maintains coordinated flight.
3. Applies the necessary wind-drift corrections to track a constant radius turn around the selected reference point.
6. Maintains the desired altitude, ± 100 feet.
7. Maintains the desired airspeed, ± 10 knots.

NIGHT FLIGHT OPERATIONS (AMEL)

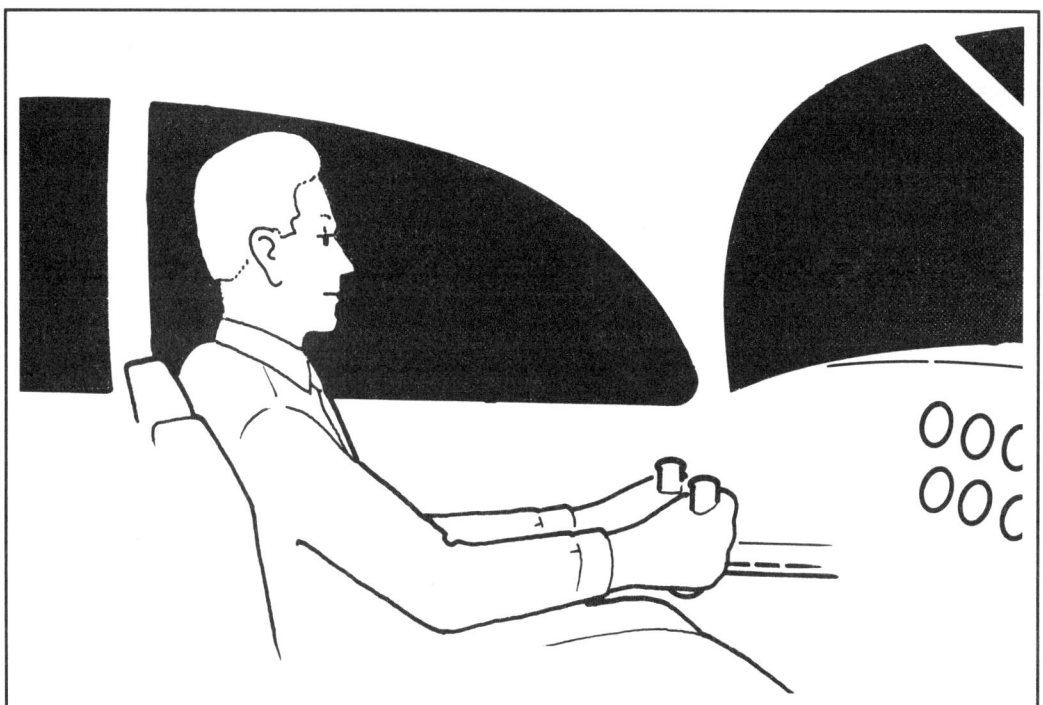

XI. AREA OF OPERATION: *NIGHT FLIGHT OPERATIONS*

NOTE: This AREA OF OPERATION is NOT required for the addition of a multiengine land class rating. However, if the applicant is to be evaluated on night flying operations, then the examiner must evaluate elements 1 through 3. Elements 4 through 8 may be evaluated at the option of the examiner.

Night flight operations will be evaluated ONLY if the applicant meets night flying regulatory requirements. If this AREA OF OPERATION is not evaluated, the applicant's certificate will bear the limitation "Night Flying Prohibited."

A. TASK: NIGHT FLIGHT

PILOT OPERATION — 9

REFERENCES: AC 61-21, AC 67-2.

Objective. To determine that the applicant:

1. Explains preparation, equipment, and factors essential to night flight.
2. Determines airplane, airport, and navigation lighting.
3. Exhibits knowledge by explaining night flying procedures, including safety precautions and emergency actions.
4. Inspects the airplane by following the checklist which includes items essential for night flight operations.

A. TASK: NIGHT FLIGHT *(continued)*

5. Starts, taxies, and performs pretakeoff check adhering to good operating practices.
6. Performs takeoffs and climbs with emphasis on visual references.
7. Navigates and maintains orientation under VFR conditions.
8. Approaches and lands adhering to good operating practices for night flight operations.

EMERGENCY OPERATIONS

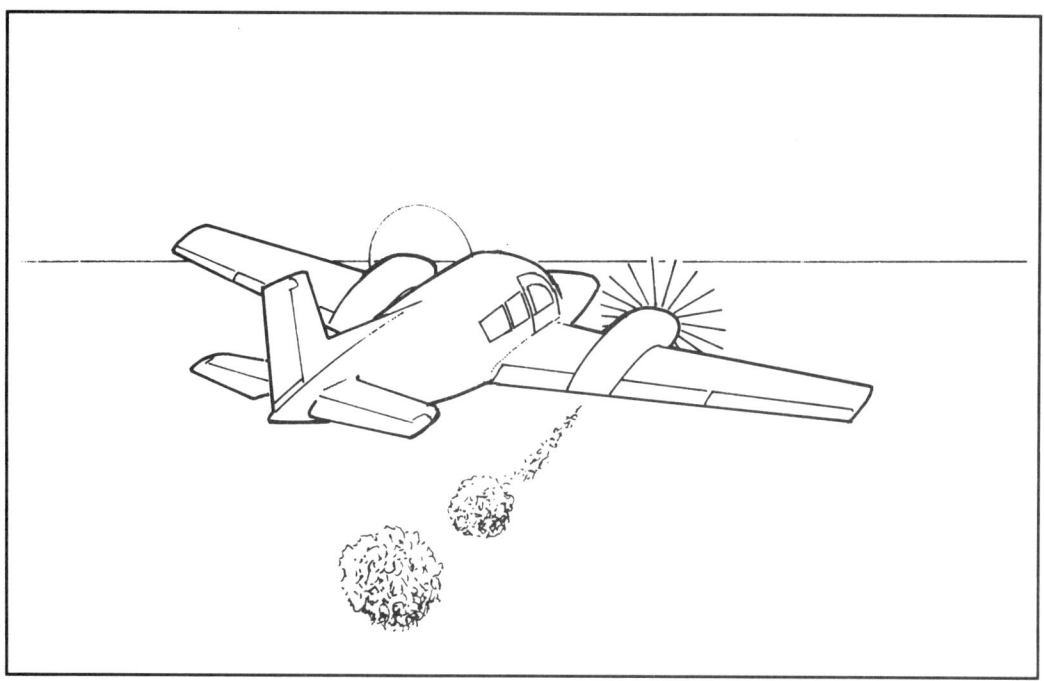

XII. AREA OF OPERATION: EMERGENCY OPERATIONS

A. TASK: SYSTEM AND EQUIPMENT MALFUNCTIONS
PILOT OPERATION — 10

REFERENCES: AC 61-21; Airplane Handbook and Flight Manual.

Objective. To determine that the applicant:

1. Exhibits knowledge by explaining causes of, indications of, and pilot actions for malfunctions of various systems and equipment.
2. Takes appropriate action for simulated emergencies such as —
   (a) partial power loss.
   (b) engine roughness or overheat.
   (c) loss of oil pressure.
   (d) carburetor or induction icing.
   (e) fuel starvation.
   (f) engine compartment fire.
   (g) electrical system malfunction.
   (h) hydraulic system malfunction.
   (i) landing gear or wing flap malfunction.
   (j) door opening in flight.
   (k) trim inoperative.
   (l) pressurization system malfunction.
   (m) other malfunctions.

B. TASK: MANEUVERING WITH ONE ENGINE INOPERATIVE

PILOT OPERATION — 10

REFERENCES: AC 61-21; Airplane Handbook and Flight Manual.

NOTE: The feathering of one propeller should be demonstrated in any multiengine airplane equipped with propellers which can be safely feathered and unfeathered in flight. Feathering for pilot flight test purposes should be performed only under such conditions and at such altitudes (no lower than 3,000 feet above the surface) and positions where safe landings on established airports can be readily accomplished in the event difficulty is encountered in unfeathering. At altitudes lower than 3,000 feet above the surface, simulated engine failure will be performed by throttling the engine to idle, then to zero thrust.

A propeller that cannot be unfeathered during the practical test should be treated as an emergency.

Objective: To determine that the applicant:

1. Exhibits knowledge by explaining the flight characteristics and controllability associated with maneuvering with one engine inoperative.
2. Sets the engine controls, reduces drag, identifies and verifies the inoperative engine after simulated engine failure.
3. Attains the best engine inoperative airspeed and trims the airplane.
4. Maintains control of the airplane.
5. Attempts to determine the reason for the engine malfunction.
6. Follows the prescribed checklist to verify procedures for securing the inoperative engine.
7. Establishes a bank toward the operating engine, as required for best performance.
8. Turns toward the nearest suitable airport.
9. Monitors the operating engine and makes necessary adjustments.
10. Demonstrates coordinated flight with one engine inoperative (propeller feathered, if possible), including —
    (a) straight-and-level flight.
    (b) turns in both directions.
    (c) descents to assigned altitudes.
    (d) climb to assigned altitudes, if airplane is capable of climbs under existing conditions.
11. Maintains the desired altitude, ± 100 feet, when a constant altitude is specified, and levels off from climbs and descents, ± 100 feet.
12. Maintains the desired heading during straight flight, ± 10 degrees.
13. Maintains the specified bank angle, ± 5 degrees, during turns.
14. Divides attention between coordinated control, flightpath, and orientation.
15. Demonstrates engine restart in accordance with prescribed procedures.

EMERGENCY OPERATIONS (AMEL)

C. TASK: ENGINE INOPERATIVE LOSS OF DIRECTIONAL CONTROL DEMONSTRATION

PILOT OPERATION — 10

REFERENCES: AC 61-21; Airplane Handbook and Flight Manual.

NOTE: There is a density altitude above which the stalling speed is higher than the engine inoperative minimum control speed. When this density altitude exists close to the ground because of high elevations and/or high temperatures, and effective flight demonstration of loss of directional control may be hazardous and should not be attempted. If it is determined prior to flight that the stall speed is higher than Vmc and this flight demonstration is impracticable, the significance of the engine inoperative minimum control speed should be emphasized through oral testing, including the results of attempting engine inoperative flight below this speed, the recognition of loss of directional control, and proper recovery techniques.

The engine inoperative loss of directional control demonstration should be performed at an altitude from which recovery from loss of control can be safely made. Recovery should be initiated by simultaneously reducing power on the operating engine and reducing the angles of attack by lowering the nose. If a stall occurs prior to reaching Vmc, recovery should be initiated immediately by reducing the angle of attack.

Recoveries should never be made by increasing power on the simulated failed engine.

The practice of entering this maneuver by increasing pitch attitude to a high point with both engines operating and then reducing power on the critical engine should be avoided because the airplane may become uncontrollable when the power on the critical engine is reduced.

Objective. To determine that the applicant:

1. Exhibits knowledge by explaining the causes of loss of directional control at airspeeds less than Vmc, the factors affecting Vmc, and the safe recovery procedures.
2. Selects an entry altitude that will allow recoveries to be completed no lower than 3,000 feet AGL.
3. Establishes the airplane configuration with —
   (a) propeller set to high RPM.
   (b) landing gear retracted.
   (c) flaps set in takeoff position.
   (d) cowl flaps set in takeoff position.
   (e) engines set to rated takeoff power, or as recommended.
   (f) trim set for takeoff.
   (g) power on the critical engine reduced to idle (avoid abrupt power reduction).
4. Establishes a single engine climb attitude (inoperative engine propeller windmilling) with the airspeed representative of that following a normal takeoff.
5. Establishes a bank toward the operating engine, as required for best performance.
6. Reduces the airspeed slowly with the elevators while applying rudder pressure to maintain directional control until full rudder is applied.
7. Recognizes the indications of loss of directional control.
8. Recovers promptly by simultaneously reducing the angle of attack, and adjusts power on operating engine sufficiently to maintain control with minimum loss of altitude.
9. Recovers within 15 degrees of the entry heading.

D. TASK: DEMONSTRATING ME EFFECTS OF VARIOUS AIRSPEEDS AND CONFIGURATIONS DURING ENGINE INOPERATIVE PERFORMANCE

PILOT OPERATION — 10

REFERENCES: AC 61-21; Airplane Handbook and Flight Manual.

Objective. To determine that the applicant:

1. Exhibits knowledge by explaining the effects of various airspeeds and configurations on performance during engine-inoperative operation.
2. Selects an entry altitude that will allow recoveries to be completed no lower than 3,000 feet AGL.
3. Establishes Vyse appropriate to the altitude, with critical engine at zero thrust.
4. Varies the airspeed from Vyse and demonstrates the effect of the airspeed changes on performance.
5. Maintains Vyse, within ± 5 knots and heading, ± 10 degrees, and demonstrates the effect of each of the following on performance —
   (a) clean configuration.
   (b) extension of landing gear.
   (c) extension of wing flaps.
   (d) extension of both landing gear and wing flaps.
   (e) windmilling of propeller on the critical engine.

E. TASK: ENGINE FAILURE EN ROUTE

PILOT OPERATION — 10

REFERENCE: AC 61-21.

Objective. To determine that the applicant:

1. Exhibits knowledge by explaining the techniques and procedures used if engine failure occurs while en route.
2. Sets the engine controls, reduces drag, and identifies and verifies the inoperative engine after simulated engine failure.
3. Establishes the proper power setting appropriate to the conditions.
4. Maintains control of the airplane.
5. Attempts to determine the reason for the engine malfunction.
6. Follows the prescribed checklist to verify procedures for securing the inoperative engine.

EMERGENCY OPERATIONS (AMEL)

7. Establishes a bank toward the operating engine, as required for best performance.
8. Turns toward nearest suitable airport.
9. Maintains an altitude or a minimum sink rate sufficient to continue flight, considering —
   (a) density altitude.
   (b) service ceiling.
   (c) gross weight.
   (d) elevation of terrain and obstructions.
10. Monitors the operating engine and makes necessary adjustments.
11. Maintains the desired altitude, ± 100 feet, if within the airplane capability, the desired heading, ± 10 degrees.
12. Divides attention between coordinated airplane control, flightpath, and orientation.
13. Contacts appropriate facility for assistance, if necessary.

F. TASK: ENGINE FAILURE ON TAKEOFF BEFORE Vmc

PILOT OPERATION — 10

REFERENCE: AC 61-21.

NOTE: The power reduction on an engine will be accomplished before reaching 50 percent Vmc.

Objective. To determine that the applicant:

1. Exhibits knowledge by explaining the reasons for the procedures used for engine failure on takeoff before Vmc, including related safety factors.
2. Aligns the airplane on the runway centerline.
3. Advances the throttles smoothly to maximum allowable power.
4. Checks engine instruments.
5. Maintains directional control on the runway centerline.
6. Closes throttles smoothly and promptly when simulated engine failure occurs.
7. Maintains directional control and applies braking, as necessary.

G. TASK: ENGINE FAILURE AFTER LIFT-OFF

PILOT OPERATION — 10

REFERENCE: AC 61-21.

Objective. To determine that the applicant:.

1. Exhibits knowledge by explaining the reasons for the procedures used if engine failure occurs after lift-off, including related safety factors.
2. Recognizes engine failure promptly.
3. Sets the engine controls, reduces drag, and identifies and verifies the inoperative engine after simulated engine failure.

THE COMPLETE MULTIENGINE PILOT

ENGINE FAILURE AFTER LIFT-OFF (*continued*)

4. Establishes Vyse if there are no obstructions; if obstructions are present, establishes Vxse or Vmc, + 5, whichever is greater, until obstructions are cleared, then Vyse and trims the airplane.
5. Maintains control of the airplane.
6. Follows the prescribed checklist to verify procedures for securing the inoperative engine.
7. Establishes a bank toward the operating engine, as required for best performance.
8. Recognizes the airplane performance capability; if a climb is impossible at Vyse, maintains Vyse and initiates an approach to the most suitable landing area.
9. Attempts to determine the reason for the engine malfunction.
10. Monitors the operating engine and makes necessary adjustments.
11. Maintains the desired heading, ± 10 degrees and the desired airspeed, ± 5 knots.
12. Divides attention between coordinated airplane control, flightpath, and orientation.
13. Contacts the appropriate facility for assistance, if necessary.

H. APPROACH AND LANDING WITH AN INOPERATIVE ENGINE

PILOT OPERATION — 10

REFERENCE: AC 61-21.

Objective. To determine that the applicant:

1. Exhibits knowledge by explaining the procedure used during an approach and landing with a simulated inoperative engine.
2. Sets the engine controls, reduce drag, and identifies and verifies inoperative engine after simulated engine failure.
3. Establishes the recommended airspeed, +5, -0 knots, and trims the airplane.
4. Follows the prescribed checklist to verify procedures for securing the simulated inoperative engine and completes prelanding checklist.
5. Establishes a bank toward the operating engine, as required for best performance.
6. Maintains proper track on final approach.
7. Establishes the approach and landing configuration and power.
8. Maintains a stabilized descent angle and the recommended final approach airspeed +5, -0 knots of Vyse until landing is assured.
9. Touches down smoothly beyond and within 500 feet of a specified point, with no appreciable drift and the longitudinal axis aligned with the runway centerline.
10. Maintains correct control during after-landing roll.

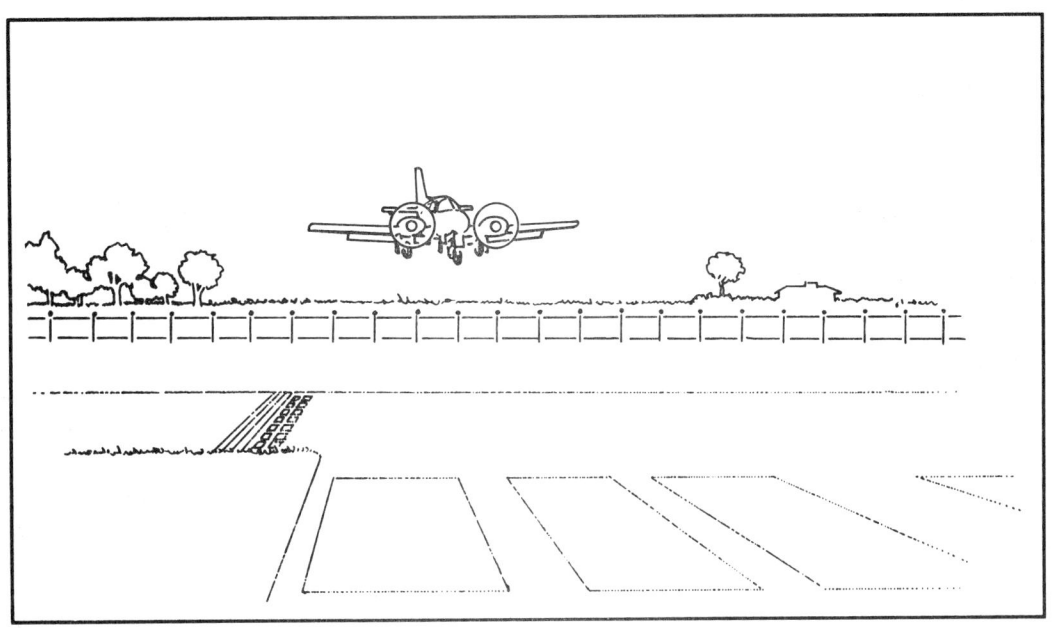

XIII. AREA OF OPERATION: APPROACHES AND LANDINGS

A. TASK: NORMAL AND CROSSWIND APPROACHES AND LANDINGS

PILOT OPERATION — 10

REFERENCE: AC 61-21.

Objective. To determine that the applicant:

1. Exhibits knowledge by explaining the elements of normal and crosswind approaches and landings, including airspeeds, configurations, crosswind limitations, and related safety factors.
2. Maintains the proper ground track on final approach.
3. Establishes the approach and landing configuration and power required.
4. Maintains a stabilized descent angle and the recommended approach airspeed, ± 5 knots.
5. Makes smooth, proper, and correct control application during final approach and transition from approach to landing roundout.
6. Touches down at or within 500 feet beyond a specified point, with no appreciable drift, and the airplane longitudinal axis aligned with the runway centerline.
7. Maintains directional control, increasing aileron deflection into the wind, as necessary, during the after-landing roll.

NOTE: If a crosswind condition does not exist, the applicant's knowledge of the TASK will be evaluated through oral testing.

B. TASK: GO-AROUND

PILOT OPERATION-5

REFERENCE: AC 61-21.

Objective. To determine that the applicant:.

1. Exhibits knowledge by explaining the elements of the go-around procedure, including proper decision, recommended airspeeds, drag effect of wing flaps and landing gear, and coping with undesirable pitch and yaw.
2. Makes a proper decision to go-around.
3. Applies takeoff power and establishes the proper pitch attitude to attain the recommended airspeed.
4. Retracts the wing flaps, as recommended, and at a safe altitude, and establishes Vy
5. Retracts the landing gear after a positive rate of climb has been established.
6. Trims the airplane and climbs at Vy, ± 5 knots, and maintains the proper track.

C. TASK: MAXIMUM PERFORMANCE APPROACH AND LANDING

PILOT OPERATION — 8

REFERENCE: AC 61-21.

Objective. To determine that the applicant:

1. Exhibits knowledge by explaining the elements of a maximum performance approach and landing, including airspeeds, configurations, and related safety factors.
2. Considers obstructions, landing surface, and wind conditions.
3. Selects a suitable touchdown point.
4. Maintains proper track on final approach.
5. Establishes the maximum performance approach and landing configuration, recommended airspeed, and descent angle.
6. Maintains a stabilized descent angle and the recommended airspeed, ± 5 knots.
7. Touches down at or within 200 feet beyond a specified point, with minimum float, no appreciable drift, and the airplane longitudinal axis aligned with the runway centerline.
8. Maintains directional control during after-landing roll.
9. Applies braking and controls, as recommended, to stop in the shortest distance consistent with safety.

PRACTICAL TEST CHECKLIST (AMEL)

(SUGGESTED)

APPLICANT'S NAME _____

EXAMINER'S NAME _____

DATE _____

TYPE CHECK _____

I. PREFLIGHT PREPARATION

- ❏ A. Certificates And Documents
- ❏ B. Obtaining Weather Information
- ❏ C. Cross-Country Flight Planning

II. MULTIENGINE OPERATION

- ❏ A. Airplane Systems
- ❏ B. Emergency Procedures
- ❏ C. Normal Procedures
- ❏ D. Determining Performance And Flight Planning
- ❏ E. Use Of Minimum Equipment List
- ❏ F. Flight Principles — Engine Inoperative
- ❏ G. Aeromedical Factors

III. GROUND OPERATIONS

- ❏ A. Visual Inspection
- ❏ B. Cockpit Management
- ❏ C. Starting Engines
- ❏ D. Taxiing
- ❏ E. Pretakeoff Check
- ❏ F. Postflight Procedures

continued on following page

PRACTICAL TEST CHECKLIST (*continued*)

IV. AIRPORT AND TRAFFIC PATTERN OPERATIONS

- ❏ A. Radio Communications And ATC Light Signals
- ❏ B. Traffic Pattern Operations
- ❏ C. Airport And Runway Marking And Lighting

V. TAKEOFFS AND CLIMBS

- ❏ A. Normal And Crosswind Takeoffs And Climbs
- ❏ B. Maximum Performance Takeoff and Climb

VI. CROSS-COUNTRY FLYING

- ❏ A. Pilotage And Dead Reckoning
- ❏ B. Radio Navigation
- ❏ C. Diversion
- ❏ D. Lost Procedures

VII. FLIGHT BY REFERENCE TO INSTRUMENTS

- ❏ A. Straight-and-Level Flight
- ❏ B. Straight, Constant Airspeed Climbs
- ❏ C. Straight, Constant Airspeed Descents
- ❏ D. Turns To Headings
- ❏ E. Unusual Flight Attitudes
- ❏ F. Radio Aids And Radar Services

VIII. INSTRUMENT FLIGHT

- ❏ A. Engine Failure During Straight-and-level Flight And Turns
- ❏ B. Instrument Approach — All Engines Operating
- ❏ C. Instrument Approach — One Engine Inoperative

IX. FLIGHT AT CRITICALLY SLOW AIRSPEED

- ❏ A. Imminent Stalls, Gear Up And Flaps Up
- ❏ B. Imminent Stalls, Gear Down And Full Flaps
- ❏ C. Maneuvering During Slow Flight
- ❏ D. Constant-altitude Turns

PRACTICAL TEST CHECKLIST (AMEL)

X. FLIGHT MANEUVERING BY REFERENCE TO GROUND OBJECTS

- ❏ A. Rectangular Course
- ❏ B. S-Turns Across A Road
- ❏ C. Turns Around A Point

XI. NIGHT FLIGHT OPERATIONS

- ❏ A. Night Flight

XII. EMERGENCY OPERATIONS

- ❏ A. System And Equipment Malfunctions
- ❏ B. Maneuvering With One Engine Inoperative
- ❏ C. Engine Inoperative Loss Of Directional Control Demonstration
- ❏ D. Demonstrating The Effects Of Various Airspeeds And
- ❏ Configurations During Engine Inoperative Performance
- ❏ E. Engine Failure En Route
- ❏ F. Engine Failure On Takeoff Before Vmc
- ❏ G. Engine Failure After Lift-off
- ❏ H. Approach And Landing With An Inoperative Engine

XIII. APPROACHES AND LANDINGS

- ❏ A. Normal And Crosswind Approaches And Landings
- ❏ B. Go-Around
- ❏ C. Maximum Performance Approach And Landing

APPLICANT'S PRACTICAL TEST CHECKLIST

(SUGGESTED)

APPOINTMENT WITH INSPECTOR OR EXAMINER:

NAME _____

TIME/DATE _____

ACCEPTABLE AIRCRAFT

- ❏ View-Limiting Device (if applicable)
- ❏ Aircraft Documents:
- ❏ Airworthiness Certificate
- ❏ Registration Certificate
- ❏ Operating Limitations
- ❏ Aircraft Maintenance Records: Airworthiness Inspections
- ❏ FCC Station License

PERSONAL EQUIPMENT

- ❏ Current Aeronautical Charts
- ❏ Computer and Plotter
- ❏ Flight Plan Form
- ❏ Flight Logs
- ❏ Current AIM

PERSONAL RECORDS

- ❏ Pilot Certificate
- ❏ Medical Certificate
- ❏ Completed FAA Form 8710-1, Airman Certificate and/or Rating Application
- ❏ AC Form 8080-2, Airman Written Test Report
- ❏ Logbook with Instructor's Endorsement
- ❏ Notice of Disapproval (if applicable)
- ❏ Approved School Graduation Certificate (if applicable)
- ❏ FCC Radiotelephone Operator Permit (if applicable)
- ❏ Examiner's Fee (if applicable)

THE COMPLETE MULTIENGINE PILOT

Appendix C

INDEX FOR
THE COMPLETE MULTIENGINE PILOT

Accelerate-stop distance	4-13
Accelerate-go distance	4-14
Accumulators	3-3
Air starts	3-3
Alternate air source	3-6
Altitude; cruise	6-2
Best angle of climb	4-10
Best rate of climb	4-10
Braking	7-5
Climb gradient	5-3
Combustion heaters	3-15
Cowl flaps	3-4, 6-1
Critical engine	2-5
Critical altitude	3-10
Crossfeed	5-8
Cruise power tables	4-17
Cruise altitude	6-2
Descent planning	4-18
Drag, induced	2-2
Drag, minimum	2-2
Drag, parasitic	2-2
Drag; flat-plate	4-8
Drift down	6-5
EGT	3-4
Electrical systems	3-8
Emergency exits	3-19
Environmental system	3-14
Excess horsepower	2-1
Feathering sequence	5-6
Flat plate drag	4-8, 7-3
Fuel injection	3-5
Fuel systems	3-7
Fuel management	6-1
Heaters, combustion	3-15
Horsepower, excess	2-1
Hydroplaning	7-5
Ice protection	3-17
Induced drag	2-2
Intercoolers	3-12
Intersection takeoffs	5-4
Landing gear extension	3-13, 7-6
Landing distance	7-4
Lateral balance	4-5
Leaning	6-3
Light twin	2-3
Minimum Safe Single-Engine Speed	4-10
Minimum Controllable Airspeed	4-9
Mixture control	6-3
Normally aspirated	3-10
Overboosting	3-11
Parasitic drag	2-2
Power loading	2-1, 4-1
Pressurization	3-13
Propeller synchronizers	3-4
Propeller governor	3-2
Propeller blade angle	3-1
Propeller pitch	3-1
P-factor	2-4
Range and endurance	4-16
Securing sequence	5-6
Slip/skid indicator	2-6
Stalls	8-4
Structural icing	3-17

Takeoff distance 4-12	V_{no} 4-11
Time, fuel, and distance 4-15	V_{sse} 4-10
Turbocharging 3-10	V_x 4-10
Unfeathering accumulators 3-3	V_{xse} 4-11
V_a 4-11	V_y 4-10, 4-11
Vacuum system 3-16	V_{yse} 4-11
V_{le} 4-10	Yaw string 2-6, 5-5
V_{lo} 4-10	Zero thrust 2-2, 7-2
V_{mc} 4-9	Zero fuel weight 4-2
V_{ne} 4-11	Zero sideslip 2-6, 5-5